$1.95 EACH—WESTERN TRAVEL BOOKS FROM WARD RITCHIE PRESS

Trips for the Day or Week end

ALL BOOKS COMPLETE WITH M

QUANTITY

☐ **EXPLORING CALIFORNIA BYWAYS, #1** Mexican Border $_____

☐ **EXPLORING CALIFORNIA BYWAYS, #2** In ...... Los Angeles $_____

☐ **EXPLORING CALIFORNIA BYWAYS, #3** Desert Country $_____

☐ **EXPLORING CALIFORNIA BYWAYS, #4** Mountain Country $_____

☐ **EXPLORING CALIFORNIA BYWAYS, #5** Historic Sites of California $_____

☐ **A GUIDEBOOK TO THE LAKE TAHOE COUNTRY** $_____

☐ **A GUIDEBOOK TO THE MOJAVE DESERT OF CALIFORNIA,** Including Death Valley, Joshua Tree National Monument, and the Antelope Valley $_____

☐ **A GUIDEBOOK TO THE MOUNTAINS OF ORANGE AND SAN DIEGO COUNTIES** $_____

☐ **A GUIDEBOOK TO THE NORTHERN CALIFORNIA COAST, VOL. I.** Highway 1 $_____

☐ **A GUIDEBOOK TO THE NORTHERN CALIFORNIA COAST, VOL. II.** Humboldt and Del Norte Counties $_____

[SEE MORE BOOKS ON OTHER SIDE]

WARD RITCHIE PRESS
3044 Riverside Drive, Los Angeles, Calif. 90039

Please send me the Western Travel Books I have checked. I am enclosing $_____, (check or money order—no currency or C.O.D.'s). Please include the list price plus 25¢ a copy and 25¢ for each additional copy to cover mailing costs.

Name _____

Address _____

City _____ State _____ Zip Code _____

GERSHON WELTMAN, left, is a scientist with a Ph.D. in Engineering and a former UCLA professor.

ELISHA DUBIN is an architect and a photographer.

Both are bicycle enthusiasts and old-time Los Angeles City buffs. They are pondering more bicycle touring books on Southern California.

Bicycling in Los Angeles offers an assortment of sights.

BICYCLE TOURING IN LOS ANGELES

BY GERSHON WELTMAN
AND ELISHA DUBIN

WARD RITCHIE PRESS · LOS ANGELES

DEDICATION

*This book is dedicated to that unsung Scotsman,
Kirkpatrick MacMillan, who in 1839 first joined pedal
to wheel for the benefit and pleasure of humanity.*

---

*The material in this book is reviewed and updated
at each printing.*

PHOTOGRAPHS AND MAP DESIGN BY *Elisha Dubin*

PREFACE

By Councilman Marvin Braude
Eleventh District, City of Los Angeles

When I was a boy and received my first bicycle it opened up a whole new world of adventure and discovery. Today, I still feel this excitement of adventure and discovery every time I ride. Even over old routes I always see something new, I never tire of the fresh air flowing past my face and the unlimited panoramas that unfold.

I'd rather ride my bicycle than drive a car. And for the short haul I get much more out of my bike. Other people must feel the same. Bicycle riding in America is at an all-time high. In fact, more people are riding in every walk of life and every age group.

The recreational benefits of bike riding are overwhelming. Bike riding can be an inexpensive family sport. With your loved ones, friends — both new and old — or alone, the experience of being reintroduced to your community from the vantage of a bicycle is exciting. Exploring new areas via a bike holds opportunities found in few other means of travel.

Physicians and health officers everywhere have prescribed the bicycle as an aid to better health — both physical and mental. As Dr. Paul Dudley White has said, "If more of us rode bicycles, we would have a sharp reduction in the use of tranquilizers and sleeping pills."

In addition, motorists are becoming disenchanted with the congestion and air pollution created by cars and trucks. Though the bike has not taken a position as a widely used commuter

5

vehicle — as it has in Europe — more and more people are getting to work on bikes.

In Los Angeles, what we need now is more legislation to permit more bicycle lanes. Creating bicycle lanes on existing streets is one approach, and a good one. Several of the routes described in this book follow such marked bikeways. On those streets, highly visible signs alert the motorist to the presence of bicycles, and make the city a safer place to tour and explore.

Countless other possibilities exist for off-street bikepaths. For example, utility rights of way usually contain no more than barren earth, perhaps linear weed patches or grass. Frequently, with little effort and expense, a right of way can be turned into a bike path. Existing pathways in parks or on parkways can also be assigned to bicycle use and, if so marked, can be safely used. Flood control channels, river banks, abandoned or little used railroad rights of way, and rural fire lanes also hold a potential for bike use.

Those communities that may be reluctant to procede with any of these possibilities need merely observe what has been done elsewhere. Huge cities and small towns across America have acted to improve urban and suburban cycling. Few things happen spontaneously. It is important to let local officials know there is a public demand. The will of the people is seldom denied — if that will is made strong and clear.

CONTENTS

With a bicycle you can go almost anywhere . . .
beach or mountains.

INTRODUCTION

We are witnessing today the renaissance of bicycle riding in the United States. Its classical age was the 1890's, when the noble two-wheeler was perfected just as our city and country roads were finally paved. Swarms of freedom-seeking cyclists took quick advantage, greatly outnumbering the few sputtering automobiles. The automobile prevailed by promising even greater freedom. But it delivered tyranny instead. And the rebirth of cycling is surely in part a long overdue reaction to this disappointment. At last, the cyclists have returned to reclaim the roads. Or their fair share of them at least.

This book is a guide to bicycle riding for pleasure in and around the city of Los Angeles. It contains 23 tours, most of them round trips, none of them overly hard, all of them worth exploring. They are intended to lure the recreational cyclist and the cycling family beyond their neighborhood horizons into broader prospects. The tours include the few established bike-paths in the Los Angeles area. For the most part, however, the idea is to chart new routes, interesting and safe, over the streets and roads of this unique community.

And Los Angeles certainly is unique. Brash and new, it has a cultural heritage which spans over 250 years. Chided for ugliness, it contains some of the finest natural scenery and architecture of any American city. Slave to the automobile, its freeways overlie a rapid transit network that existed before cars were a major factor. Los Angeles is a subtle place which reveals itself only grudgingly. But to the cyclist it is a place of great opportunity, for awareness as well as for pleasure.

Pleasure in cycling comes in many ways. As Councilman Braude pointed out in his preface, there is a sense of adventure

9

and discovery in bicycle riding that one gets from few other everyday activities. Cycling is observation and participation together. The bicycle rider is part of the scene; there are no barriers between him and the environment. He moves fast enough to capture sizeable distances, slow enough to take in small details. Movement itself is a pleasure: the wind in the face, of course, but also the silent rhythmic flow over rolling terrain, and, downhill flights as exciting as any ski run.

Perhaps the greatest pleasure, though, is that of achievement. Cycling brings to everyone the exhilaration of going the distance or making the hill, the satisfaction of skill in balance, in a nicely executed gear change, even in a well-planned trip. Like the hiker, the cyclist earns his route. Once ridden, it is his, in a way no motorized tourist will ever know.

What we have tried to do in laying out these tours is to bring the various pleasures of cycling to the exploration of Los Angeles, the city. To us, the effort was most rewarding. Los Angeles by bicycle became a much richer environmental experience. We gained a far better appreciation of its geography, its history, and its culture. Hopefully, this guide will help make these discoveries more readily available to our fellow cyclists.

How did we select our tours? We began, as most such projects begin, in disorganization, with a sampling of our own favorite rides, those of others, a long list of places to include for various reasons, and the idea that for convenience, the rides should by and large be close to where the people are. As we plotted our first collection of tours on a large area map, a pattern emerged. We found that the truly worthwhile tours fell into three characteristic environments. These were:

The City. From downtown west to Santa Monica runs the civic spine of Los Angeles. This is where the city developed from an adobe pueblo to a major population center, and where the main functions of government, commerce, and culture are carried out. Bicycle touring here is a fascinating exploration of the urban environment. The cyclist moves through neighborhoods rich and poor, new and old, straight and hip, examining the architecture of streets, of buildings, and of homes, visiting the special districts, the centers, the parks and the people that make up the dynamic metropolis.

The Coast. The vast body of Los Angeles is sustained by river water, from the Colorado, the Owens, and the Feather; but her soul is fed by the blue Pacific Ocean. Touring the coast from Malibu to Los Alamitos Bay, the cyclist explores first hand the close connection between the city and the sea. Broad lovely beaches, magnificent palisades, picturesque seaside communities, piers and marina, harbor and docks, are all part of this ideal environment for bicycle riding.

The Foothills and Valleys. The flatlands of Los Angeles give rise to mountains which would be the major attraction of many a small country. Even old-time residents are startled, when the smog clears, to find these rugged intruders in their midst. Along the gentle foothills of the Santa Monicas, the Simis, the Santa Susannas and the San Gabriels, the cyclist finds rides of great scenic beauty and historical interest, and communities as different as the Western charm of Calabasas is from the affluent splendor of Pasadena and San Marino. Challenges are there as well, if desired, tests of muscles and lungs against the mountain passes and upper slopes.

Three environments, three kinds of cycling experience, each different, each enjoyable, available the year round. Not forgetting the smog, considering the traffic, taking into account the urban blight and the tawdriness, still, the bicycle rider in Los Angeles

11

has much to be thankful for. And when the air is clear, which it is more often than we realize, cycling here can be glorious indeed.

We chose the tours in each environment to be representative, to be scenic, to be as safe as possible, and above all, to be interesting. A good deal of attention was paid to architecture, because bicycle riding is so visual, and because architecture tells us so much about the city, past and present. Many of the rides are easy enough for the youngest cyclist, or the newest one. None of them is really beyond reach of the average, healthy person who rides once in a while on weekends.

We left out much, of course. The endless industrial flatlands of southeast Los Angeles were ignored, to no great loss. But other more interesting areas might have been included if we had had more room. Perhaps a later edition will describe them, along with the many fine rides in the surrounding countryside which we also had to neglect.

In any case, there are enough rides in this collection to keep a cyclist busy for quite a while. All are long enough to make a pleasant outing; most are planned for an excursion of a half-day or more. Frequently, the routes adjoin, so that enthusiastic riders can put two or more together to make longer tours. Together, they offer a set of experiences, and a view of our multifaceted Los Angeles, attainable by no other means.

How do you use the book? First you choose a tour. Most cyclists will want to begin with a ride close to home, well within their capacity, perhaps with minimal traffic. Later, plan to wander further afield, taking longer rides of various types. Our tour descriptions provide some vital statistics about the ride, and summarize, if all too briefly, its character and the main points of interest. Some rides are best made at certain times of year, and this should also be considered.

The tour chosen, review the route. Places of special interest are numbered on the map, and described by short notes in the section called Along the Way. If several people are riding — and group tours are the most fun — arrange a starting place and time. Put your vehicle in shape, prepare clothing and refreshment, and be off.

Since the tours are only suggested routes, the cyclist should feel free to experiment. Make the ride in the opposite direction if you want to, cut it short if you have to. Explore the "uncharted" areas off the main track. For some of the hillier rides, downhill "bail-out" routes have been purposefully included to allow a tired cyclist to get back to the lowlands.

Several of the books that we found useful in planning the tours might increase your enjoyment of them. *A Guide to Architecture in Southern California* (Los Angeles County Museum of Art), by David Gebhard and Robert Winter, has many fine short descriptions of our better buildings. An Englishman, Reyner Banham, has written the most perceptive and cheering book about our confusing city that we have yet encountered. Called *Los Angeles: The Architecture of Four Ecologies,* it contains much relevant historical and social comment; Harper and Row is the publisher. And of course, as a final arbiter of passageways and alleys, there is the 1971 Edition of *The Los Angeles Popular Street Atlas,* published by Thomas Bros. Maps.

The rest is in the book and on the road. Have fun, be careful, and . . . ride on!

HINTS ON BICYCLE TOURING

Touring by bicycle is likely to be a new experience for some of our readers. It is mainly for this group that we have assembled these few hints on the bicycle and how to use it. Nevertheless, the more experienced rider may also learn something of value.

Choosing A Bicycle. Not so many years ago, an adult looking for a bicycle at the old neighborhood shop would be offered, with apologies, a few sad and dusty vehicles which may have made their ocean voyage before the great wars. Today, one is pointed toward a gleaming array of precision machinery, neatly arranged in a brightly-lit emporium. For the average recreational cyclist, however, the choice of a suitable bicycle is not as difficult as might appear. The important thing is to recognize the proper class of bike. After that, the only problem is price, a minor matter at best.

We recommend a 10-speed lightweight for the kind of touring described in this book. It should have dropped handle bars for efficiency, good center-pull brakes, and if possible, trap pedals. (Your local purveyor will explain these esoteric terms). A hard and narrow saddle is painful at first, but soon becomes more comfortable on long rides than the wide, mushy kind. Quick-disconnect wheels are a luxury, but quite handy if you plan to transport the bike in a car trunk. Many women now prefer the stronger men's bicycle, although traditionalists can still find open-frame machines with the above features.

Bicycles of this type are made by several first-class manufacturers, the best known being our home-grown Schwinn, Raleigh of England, Peugeot of France, and American Eagle of Japan. A completely satisfactory bicycle can be bought for between $90 and $120. Above that, prices jump rapidly to about $180, then to $350 and up. The extra costs are for superlightweight construction and lower rolling friction, which are essential for the racer, but not really necessary for the casual rider. One can never lose by buying up, however, and little else will bring as much value for money, or as much pleasure.

Accessories. Keep your accessories strictly functional, bicycles are too beautiful to hang with junk. You will need a bag to carry lunches, extra clothing, camera, this book, and so forth. There are special touring bags which attach to the handlebars rather than to the saddle, these are very convenient for getting at maps and guides en route. A water bottle helps considerably on hot days. We do without a tire pump, but some people swear by them. A small kit of bike tools is also useful. Even with a rear reflector and strong front light, night riding is dangerous: but without them it is suicidal. Finally, invest in a pair of proper chamois-lined bicycling shorts. One concentrates so much better on the passing scene when freed of chafing, rubbing, and general posterior discomfort.

Upkeep. Complex as it seems, the modern 10-speed touring bicycle is really quite a rugged piece of hardware, and rarely needs adjustment. Keep it clean, keep it oiled and greased, and it may well last forever.

Maintenance can be learned from your supplier, or from various books on the bicycle. One of the best, and cheapest, is a pamphlet put out by the Los Angeles Earth Action Council. Called simply *The Bicycle Book,* it gives step-by-step directions for simple upkeep, and for more complicated repair jobs as well. The average cyclist, however, will want to establish friendly relations with a neighborhood bike repair shop.

Transport. A bumper rack is the most convenient way to transport your bicycle by car. For many years, only one style was available in Los Angeles. Now there are several, including some fancy models which fold flat when not in use. The better ones do not require a wrench for attachment. A standard rack holds two cycles, so that transporting a family's equipment can get sticky without a van or pickup. We have put two childrens' cycles inside a station wagon and hung two more on an outside rack. We have also seen such arrangements as racks built one atop the other, a roof rack combined with a bumper rack, and bumper racks mounted front and rear. In any case, some ingenuity is necessary. Luckily, that's what built America.

Survival in Traffic. Bicycling in the city is like any other risky activity. A reasonable amount of apprehension is useful, an overriding fear is dangerous. So the cyclist must work to overcome the nervousness which comes from venturing into the stream of two-ton juggernauts. Cycling cool comes from experience and from firm resolution. Remember, part of the road is rightfully yours, and can be occupied in safety.

Aside from the standard traffic rules, there is one important thing the cyclist must know. This is that most motorists have, in medical terms, a severe perceptual-motor handicap. Despite the growth of cycling, the average driver still does not expect to see a bicycle on the road, and is unsure what to do when he does see one. Consequently, drivers often act as if the cyclist is invisible, not out of malice, but out of habit.

The safe cyclist makes up for the driver's deficiencies by never taking him for granted, and never doing the unusual or unexpected. This requires constant attention at first, but soon becomes second nature. Act as if you belong, don't force the driver to think, avoid streets which are both fast and crowded, and city bicycling can be as safe, if not safer, than city motoring.

I HANCOCK PARK TO DOWNTOWN

LENGTH: *16½ miles round trip*
TERRAIN: *Mainly flat*
TRAFFIC: *Medium to heavy*
BEST RIDDEN: *Any time of the year*

This tour cuts through westside Los Angeles the way an archeologist cuts through a city mound, exposing many layers of history and social change. Our first slice, down Wilshire to its source, is one of the most gratifying. The Boulevard is named after an early developer, the eccentric millionaire-socialist Gaylord Wilshire. But it was A. W. Ross who set its tone. In 1928, Ross developed the "Miracle Mile" between Fairfax and La Brea as a classy alternative to downtown shopping. He accommodated his newly motorized customers with convenient rear parking, and the zoning laws by building only for substantial clients. This trend continued, giving us today an exciting succession of good buildings and a surprisingly uncrowded ride. Downtown, we visit first the City's origin in El Pueblo de Los Angeles, and then a little known collection of handsome "gingerbread" houses from the 1890's. After the Victorian period, Los Angeles began to spread, and the single-family California bungalow was a main factor in the population movement. Our route goes through the idyllic Echo Park district, and past an even better preserved bungalow neighborhood on Coronado Street to the west. The last leg traverses quiet Hancock Park, home of the rich for over forty years, and deposits us near Park La Brea Towers, one of the first planned high-rise communities. A fine ride, and a thought-provoking introduction to the real Los Angeles.

Along the Way

1. Hancock Park has so many attractions you may not want to leave. So we suggest you push off immediately from the east parking lot, leaving time to explore the fossil pits, the Art Museum, and the park greens when you come back.

2. Wilshire Boulevard is where one takes out-of-town visitors to show them that we can do things well in Los Angeles too. On a smogless morning, it is one of the finest city rides. Buildings of particular interest include the Prudential Insurance Company at Hauser, Wilshire Temple below Western, the Ambassador Hotel below Normandie, and Bullocks Wilshire at Vermont.

3. MacArthur Park is a pleasant spot to recoup at the edge of the downtown district. This is a gathering place for old people, and there are perpetual discussions around the small lake.

4. At Grand Avenue, we may either pick up Tour 2, the circle tour of Downtown, or take 6th Street and then Main directly to the Central Plaza. Main Street is skid row, and casts an amused if somewhat redrimmed eye on the bicycle tourist.

5. El Pueblo de Los Angeles is our half-way point, and a good place to collect some early Los Angeles history. After a snack in Olvera Street (the tacquito stands are the best value), visit the restored fire station, the Pico House hotel, and the Plaza Church at 535 North Main.

6. Sunset Boulevard starts its long and varied trek to the sea at the Plaza. Our present freeway system began with the Downtown interchange, visible from Sunset and Figueroa.

7. We turn off Sunset at Marion Avenue and take Edgeware Road up to Carroll Avenue. In the 1890's, this was an exclusive neigh-

Echo Park Bocci Ball players perpetuate an old world tradition.

The careful bicyclist can carry his fishing rod along with him.

borhood called Angelino Heights. Now, with Bunker Hill gone, it is the last cluster of Victorian homes and mansions close to the original civic center.

8. The Echo Park district remains uniquely country-like while literally a shout away from Downtown. An amalgam of white, oriental and chicano residents, the neighborhood may have enough vitality to survive in character. Angelus Temple, at Park and Glendale, was built in 1923 for the famous woman evangelist Aimee Semple MacPherson.

9. Coronado Street has many good examples of the California bungalow. Neat frame and stone houses like these helped spread the single-family dwelling through Los Angeles in the early century. Their design owes much to the larger houses built around 1900 by the Greene brothers in Pasadena (See Tour 7).

10. Tommy's at Beverly and Rampart is a Los Angeles landmark which also serves the tastiest chiliburgers in town.

11. At Occidental and 6th is one of those strikingly beautiful effects that a city can sometimes achieve. The gothic church on the corner is perfectly mirrored from across the street by the reflective CNA Building, itself bordered by a lovely green park.

12. Hancock Park is an affluent neighborhood, and 4th Street takes us through the middle of it. The route is appropriately decorous, lined with a number of grand houses in the Spanish style. Plans are underway to make 4th Street part of a marked bikeway from the ocean to Downtown.

13. If you are up to it, have a go at exploring Park La Brea Towers before returning to home base. Begun before World War II, and finished right after, this pioneering complex helped high-rise replace garden apartments as the most desirable upper class digs.

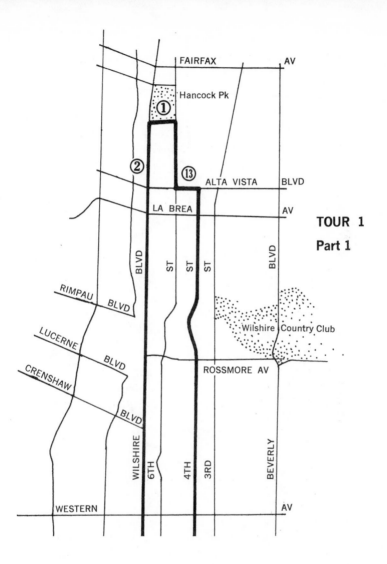

FAIRFAX AV

Hancock Pk ①

② ⑬ ALTA VISTA BLVD

LA BREA AV

TOUR 1
Part 1

BLVD

ST ST ST

BLVD

RIMPAU BLVD

Wilshire Country Club

LUCERNE BLVD

CRENSHAW

BLVD

ROSSMORE AV

WILSHIRE 6TH 4TH 3RD

BEVERLY

WESTERN AV

0   1   MILE

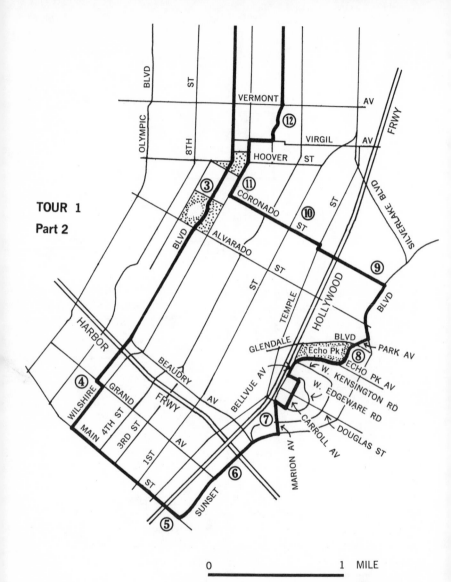

TOUR 1
Part 2

2 DOWNTOWN LOS ANGELES

LENGTH: *8 mile round trip*
TERRAIN: *Mainly flat, a few hills*
TRAFFIC: *Medium to heavy*
BEST RIDDEN: *Any time of the year*

For years, Downtown has been the most maligned part of our much maligned city. A common complaint was that it didn't exist at all. But this exaggeration only reflected what little attention people paid the familiar blur along the freeway. Now both outlook and skyline have changed. Downtown is moving again. Old sites are being restored, new buildings are going up, and much attention is being given to planning what to do with the increasing congestion. It is a good time to take a look around, and a particularly good way to do it is by bicycle. Our tour begins where Los Angeles began, in the newly revitalized Pueblo de Los Angeles. The route takes in several different aspects of the Downtown scene: ethnic life in Little Tokyo and Chinatown, government in civic center, culture on Bunker Hill, business and buildings all over. It is a short trip, but a full one, which should lead the cyclist to explore further on his own. We might suggest the train yards along Alameda Street, the eastside garment center, and the produce district around 9th and San Pedro, but everybody will have to find his own treasures. Downtown is most alive during business hours, and if you can stand the traffic, this is the time to tour. For most cyclists, however, the quiet Sunday streets will be a greater inducement.

23

Along the Way

1. El Pueblo de Los Angeles. After years of neglect, the Plaza area has come to life again as a State Historical Park, and restoration is well under way. Besides the central bandstand, places to visit include Pico House, the firehouse and the Mission Church. Olvera Street is a tourist spot, but a very nice one. The buildings are truly old, the shop owners friendly, and the tacquitos always delicious.

2. We move up a block to Spring Street and sail blightly on through Civic Center. To your left, City Hall; directly ahead, the Los Angeles Times Building.

3. Little Tokyo lies east on 1st Street between Los Angeles and Alameda Streets. This is the largest and most colorful of the several Japanese centers in Los Angeles. Rumor has it that the Atomic Cafe, at 422 East 1st Street, serves the best noodles with sauce in town.

4. The Bradbury Building, at 304 South Broadway, is Downtown's architectural surprise package. A meek, mild-mannered exterior conceals a central well of fantastic castiron balconies, stairs, and open elevators. It was designed by George H. Wyman in 1893. Across Broadway the ornate Million Dollar Theater, built as part of the Grauman's chain, shows the best in Spanish-language movies.

5. Once the Angel's Flight climbed Bunker Hill at Hill Street and Third. Now the funky funicular is in storage awaiting a promised resurrection. In the vast Central Market across the way, you can still bargain for your meat and produce, however.

Savory sweets abound aplenty on Olvera Street.

The Plaza band stand in the older part of Los Angeles
opposite Olvera Street.

6. Pershing Square is the outpost of Downtown's classier section (Park densions excepted, of course). Directly across is the venerable Biltmore Hotel, to the west and south is the emerging financial center of the whole Pacific basin.

7. At the southern end of our route lies the new Convention and Exhibition Center, designed by Charles Luckman and Associates. The main hall is as big as three football fields. A helicopter is probably a better vehicle than a bicycle for viewing this gigantic complex.

8. Flower Street is the main artery of new high-rise Downtown. The twin 52-story towers of the Atlantic-Richfield Plaza, at 6th Street, include a park-like mall and underground shopping center. From 6th and Hope Streets, we get a fine view of the Main Library, perhaps the best remaining example of how Los Angeles uniquely adapted 1920's modern to its own taste.

9. We take the narrow lane just beyond 5th Street to avoid the steepest part of Grand Avenue and climb to the shaved top of Bunker Hill. On our left are the Bunker Hill Towers, a new apartment development intended to bring people back to the central city to live as well as to work.

10. Our route brings us to the Music Center on a level with the pavillions, pools and the impressive Jacque Lipschitz sculpture, "Peace on Earth." From the east side of the promenade, there is a fine view down the Civic Mall to City Hall.

11. A moving wall of water highlights the Fort Moore Memorial on Hill Street. The cyclist and occasional pedestrian are entranced and stop to stare, but the motorist cannot risk this luxury.

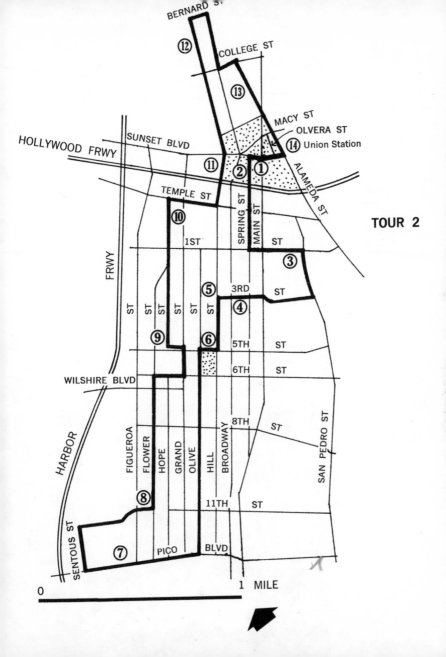

12. North Hill Street leads us to Chinatown, the real center of the Chinese community, as well as a tourist attraction. Watch for the halls of the family associations, long a major force in Chinese affairs here.

13. Phillipe's on 1001 North Alameda is a famous old eatery which claims to have invented the French Dip Sandwich.

14. Union Station is well worth seeing. Its present emptiness emphasizes the basic dignity of this massive Spanish Revival structure. The courtyards are particularly good, also the tilework and stone floors. Wouldn't this be a fine place for a restaurant and shopping center like Ghirardelli Square in San Francisco?

The architecture of the Los Angeles Music Center complex is unusual, exciting.

3 EXPOSITION PARK TO WATTS TOWERS

LENGTH: *19 miles round trip*
TERRAIN: *Flat all the way*
TRAFFIC: *Light to medium*
BEST RIDDEN: *During Watts Summer Festival*

This tour takes us from Exposition Park, home of the Los Angeles Coliseum and several of our most interesting museums, through the University of Southern California, into a fascinating section of grand 1890's homes, and on to Watts Towers, an internationally acclaimed piece of folk sculpture. We approach the towers through the black ghetto. In Los Angeles, as in other big cities, the blacks live in what the whites left behind. Fortunately perhaps, here the whites left behind single-family homes, so that there is no tenement crowding, as in the East. The depression of the ghetto, however, is measured by the almost complete lack of new buildings or major commerce, its isolation by the absence of any non-blacks on the miles of streets. In 1965, ghetto frustration and anger exploded, making Watts a household word at last. Scars of the burning can still be seen along our route. But out of the ashes came also the Watts Summer Festival, to celebrate the strength, the culture, and the contributions of this community. Each year, the Festival presents an impressive series of musical, artistic, and dramatic events. At Festival time, Watts looks outward to the city as well as inward to itself, and the cyclist or cycling group is likely to find this tour most congenial and rewarding then.

29

Along the Way

1. Our tour starts on Exposition Boulevard, at the entrance to the Rose Garden of Exposition Park. Parking here may be hard to come by when USC is in session or there is a football game at the Coliseum, but there are large lots further west.

2. We cross Exposition Boulevard with care, and take University Avenue through the graceful campus of the University of Southern California. The old blends nicely with the new in the courts and buildings of this venerable institution.

3. From the northern edge of campus we see the great Moorish dome of the Shrine Auditorium looming over the nearby buildings. Once a center of culture in Los Angeles, this massive 1925 hall is well worth the short side trip down Jefferson Boulevard.

4. On Hoover Street, we ride through a desolate reconstruction zone to enter a pleasant neighborhood of student apartments, with an occasional turn-of-the century home to remind us of its former elegance. Turning down Adams Boulevard we pass, on the way to Scharff Street, the exotic, neo-classical headquarters of the 2nd Church of Christ, Scientist.

5. A half block up Scharff we turn right into a residential park, secluded and heavily-wooded, which 75 years ago was one of the best addresses in the city. The homes on Chester Place, now owned by next door Mount St. Mary's College, illustrate perfectly the proud architecture of the 1890's.

6. Returning to Adams, we stop at the corner of Figueroa to admire St. Vincents Church, a particularly good expression of Spanish theme in a modern structure. It was designed by Albert C. Martin in 1923. Notice the beautiful tiled dome.

*The Watts Towers; Simon Rodia's extraordinary
folk sculpture.*

7. Past Santa Barbara Boulevard, Broadway enters the black precincts of Los Angeles. For over five miles, it is a lively market street of food stores, dry goods shops, newsstands, storefront churches, self-help organizations, and other small businesses.

8. At Century Boulevard the route leads us into Watts proper and past Will Rogers Memorial Park, center of activities for the annual Watts Festival. From the park we wheel down Central Avenue, turning at 108th and then at Willowbrook to find the famous towers on an isolated strip of 107th Street.

9. Watts Towers were the dream fulfilled of Simon Rodia, an Italian immigrant who labored for years to build "something big" for his adopted city. As we are drawn into his fantasy structures, we sense the vigor associated with the primitive art form: bits of color and chicken wire and stucco and steel that lift the imagination above the surrounding reality.

10. Our return to Exposition Park is up Hoover Street, a sedate and mainly residential thoroughfare. These bungalow neighborhoods were built in the 1930's when the Watts area was a center of the great electric train network which covered Los Angeles.

11. Exposition Park has enough attractions to occupy the visitor for hours. We pedal into the park with the Sports Arena on our right and the Olympic Swimming Stadium on our left. Switching to the Coliseum walkway, we circle the great stadium, past the impressive pedestal entrance, until we reach the small road leading to the Museum of Natural History. Down the way is the Museum of Science and Industry, and nearby is the formal Rose Garden, through which we can walk to reach our starting place.

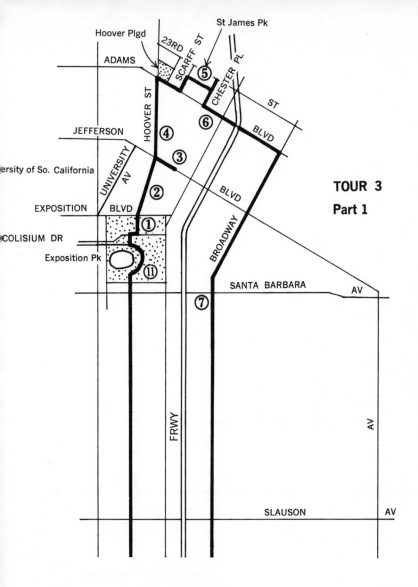

Hoover Plgd

St James Pk

23RD

SCARFF ST

ADAMS

⑤

CHESTER PL

ST

HOOVER ST

BLVD

JEFFERSON

④

③

ersity of So. California

②

UNIVERSITY

AV

BLVD

EXPOSITION

BLVD

①

COLISIUM DR

Exposition Pk

⑪

⑥

TOUR 3
Part 1

BROADWAY

SANTA BARBARA

AV

⑦

FRWY

AV

SLAUSON

AV

0   1 MILE

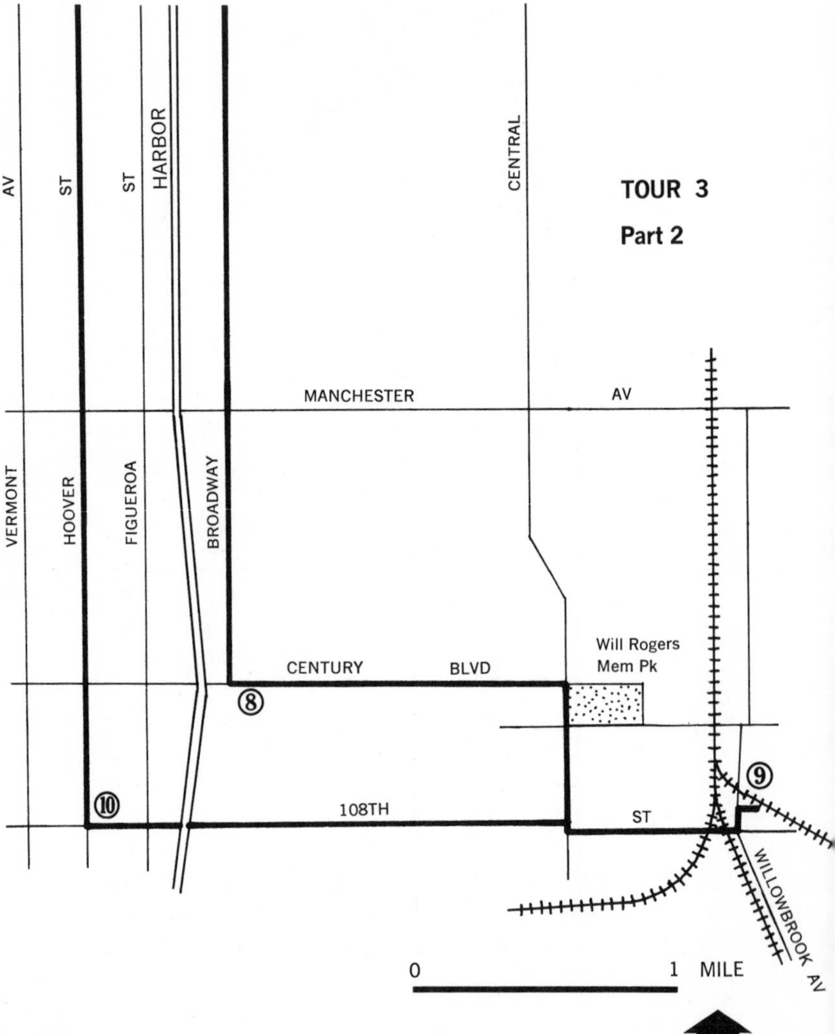

TOUR 3

Part 2

AV — VERMONT
ST — HOOVER
ST — FIGUEROA
HARBOR
BROADWAY
CENTRAL

MANCHESTER AV

CENTURY BLVD

⑧

Will Rogers
Mem Pk

⑩

108TH ST

⑨

WILLOWBROOK AV

0   1 MILE

4 ALL AROUND HOLLYWOOD

LENGTH: *13½ miles roundtrip*
TERRAIN: *Mainly flat, some mild slopes*
TRAFFIC: *Light to medium*
BEST RIDDEN: *Any time of the year*

How do you plan a bicycle tour of Hollywood? Everybody knows Hollywood isn't a place, it's a state of mind. Well, you do it in true Hollywood style. By diversion and evasion. By act instead of analysis. By riding through what purports to be Hollywood and sampling the vibrations that result. Will it be Nathaniel West or Raymond Chandler, Gore Vidal or the Chamber of Commerce? Will the ghost speak? In any case, our tour covers the ground. Fairfax, La Cienega, Hollywood, Sunset — all the famous streets. Farmer's Market, Canter's Deli, Grauman's Chinese, Radio City — all the great attractions. And more, much more besides. A look behind the glitter and tinsel at where the simple folk of Hollywood really live, or pretend to. Actually, Hollywood by bicycle is a rather good idea. People walk in Hollywood, and the whole area is oriented toward street and sidewalk. What is the cyclist but a mechanized pedestrian, after all? So he remains part of the human ebb and flow even while moving at a faster pace. And since this trip is for people and city watching, it wants to be done in a nice leisurely fashion. We recommend breakfast on Fairfax at Canter's or at DuPars in Farmer's Market, and perhaps lunch in the Art Museum when you return. There should be plenty to talk about.

35

Along the Way

1. As on Tour 1, our route starts from the parking lot on the east side of Hancock Park. The central green space is overlooked by nearby Park La Brea Towers, and the atmosphere is very much like that of Central Park in New York.

2. Right into the Towers maze we plunge, our objective is to emerge on 3rd Street at Curson Avenue, directly opposite from where we came in. The tall apartments in their meticulous grounds make any cycling group look as smart as a bicycle advertisement.

3. A short side trip on Curson Avenue leads us to the Pan Pacific Auditorium, a good example of streamlined modern from the mid 1930's. Walter Wurdeman and Welton Becket were the architects.

4. Farmer's Market is on the corner of 3rd and Fairfax Avenue. A pleasantly casual collection of eateries, produce stalls, and shops, the Market was once where local farmers sold direct to the public. Today, its fruits and vegetables are unexcelled in beauty or in price. Mostly closed Sundays.

5. CBS Television City off of Fairfax is big and impressive, but offers the cyclist little except a return stare. Built in 1952, it was designed by William Pereira and Charles Luckman.

6. Beverly and Fairfax is the gateway to the Jewish neighborhood fondly known as the Borsht Belt. Try world renowned Canter's at 419 North Fairfax for an energy-giving breakfast of lox and bagels. There are also several authentic Israeli cafes on Fairfax just above Rosewood Avenue.

*Fairfax Avenue remains the hub of a vibrant
social expression.*

7. Melrose Avenue takes us into the large district of interior decorator houses and antique shops which covers West Hollywood. We turn up La Cienega along gallery row, center of the Los Angeles fine art market. A steep hill ahead leads to the Sunset Strip, but after only a short climb, we turn back along Fountain Avenue to Fairfax, here widened into quite a thoroughfare.

8. Hollywood Boulevard begins in the foothills as a most proper residential street, but soon reveals its true raucous character. Whatever else the Boulevard is, it is undoubtedly alive. Two great landmarks of 1920's movieland pizazz are the Grauman's Chinese Theater and the Egyptian Theater, in styles to match their names, more or less.

9. Hollywood and Vine was the most famous corner in the country when everybody knew where movies and movie stars came from. The tangle of foothill streets above Franklin Avenue is still home for the Hollywood crowd, though, and its new direction is symbolized by the distinctive Capitol Records Building at the top of Vine.

10. Coming back along Sunset Boulevard we pass more momentoes of Hollywood in its heyday: CBS Radio, the Palladium, and Earl Carrolls' nightclub, now the Aquarius Theater. The classic modern of the CBS Building has dated very little, considering it was built about the same time as the Pan Pacific Auditorium.

11. Wilcox Avenue between Santa Monica and Melrose is a veritable museum of old residential Hollywood. Along with the many fine California bungalows, there are some well-preserved examples of the stucco court, sort of a horizontal apartment house popular in the 1930's, and also, at 747 North Wilcox, a great Egyptian Revival apartment, one of several built around the city.

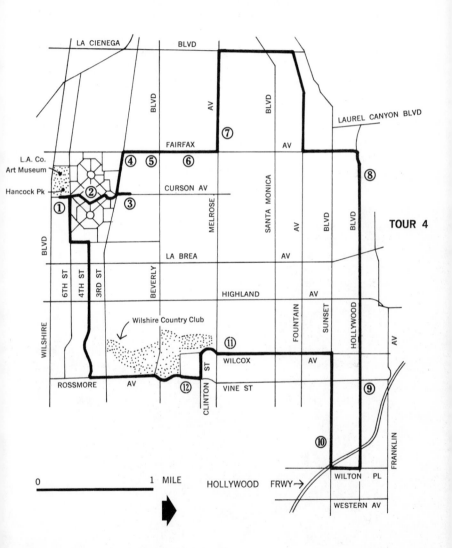

LA CIENEGA BLVD

BLVD

AV

BLVD

LAUREL CANYON BLVD

FAIRFAX ⑦ AV

L.A. Co.
Art Museum

④ ⑤ ⑥

② CURSON AV

Hancock Pk

① ③

MELROSE

SANTA MONICA

AV

BLVD

BLVD ⑧

TOUR 4

BLVD

6TH ST

4TH ST

3RD ST

BEVERLY

LA BREA

AV

HIGHLAND AV

FOUNTAIN

SUNSET

HOLLYWOOD

AV

Wilshire Country Club

WILSHIRE

⑪

ROSSMORE AV

WILCOX AV

⑫ CLINTON ST VINE ST

⑨

FRANKLIN

⑩

0   1 MILE

HOLLYWOOD   FRWY →   WILTON   PL

WESTERN AV

12. The well-mannered old brick apartment houses on Rossmore give it the fashionable look of an Eastern city. We pedal beside the Wilshire Country Club to 4th Street in the prestigious Hancock Park district, where there are many fine homes in the grand Los Angeles Spanish style. A quick detour around the Park La Brea Towers brings us back to our starting point, the County Art Museum, and the fascinating fossil pits.

Silver Lake is an urban surprise.

5 SILVER LAKE AND LOS FELIZ

LENGTH: *7½ miles round trip*
TERRAIN: *Mild slopes, a few brief hills*
TRAFFIC: *Light to medium*
BEST RIDDEN: *Any time of the year*

The Silver Lake-Los Feliz district is special in several ways. First, it is an "inner suburb," providing foothill living just minutes from Downtown. Then, it is a real neighborhood, the kind Los Angeles is supposed not to have. People have a strong feeling of belonging there, they tend to remain for uncommonly long times, and children even move back to raise their families. Finally, the district is a showcase for three of Los Angeles' most important architects: Frank Lloyd Wright, R. M. Schindler, and Richard Neutra. Wright, who was America's leading figure in architecture, designed some of his most impressive city homes for the Los Feliz foothills. Schindler and Neutra came here from Austria in the 1920's. They brought with them the new International viewpoint on simplicity and the use of space. This they adapted to local tradition, environment, and building materials. The resulting style has had a great influence on the Los Angeles cityscape. Their houses are well represented in the Silver Lake area, those of Neutra in particular. On the whole, the district is not as posh as it once was, but the scenic qualities that attracted the early home-builders have not changed. There are hills, and the cyclist must be prepared to work just a little for his architectural education, but the route is not overly hard.

41

Along the Way

1. Barnsdall Park, on the corner of Hollywood and Vermont, gives us the chance to examine a major Frank Lloyd Wright house at first hand. There is parking near the Hollywood entrance, and along the road which circles the Park knoll. Several buildings were constructed and planned for the former Barnsdall Estate. Hollyhock House, built in 1917, was Wright's first in Los Angeles, and reflects his interest in Pre-Columbian motif. It is now being restored to its original condition, as part of the Park's Municipal Arts and Crafts complex.

2. We travel down Hollywood Boulevard until it joins Sunset, which makes an almost level cut through the surrounding hills. Ducking off Sunset onto Silver Lake Boulevard, we have before us the small valley containing the lovely reservoir.

3. On the east side of the lake is Richard J. Neutra territory. His finely detailed houses look out from among the trees at an entrancing view. Neutra House at 2300 Silverlake Boulevard was the prototype. Built in 1933, it was recently restored after a fire. Others are Yew House (1957) at number 2226, Treweek House (1949) at number 2250, and Sokol House (1950) on the corner of Earl Street.

4. We carefully circumvent the steep hills west of the lake, and encounter only their lower slopes on St. George. Marshall High, on Tracy Street, is one of the city's more handsome schools. Unfortunately, it was hopelessly damaged in the 1971 quake, and is due to come down.

5. There are two houses by R. M. Schindler just over the surprise bridge on Franklin Avenue. Schlessinger House, on the corner

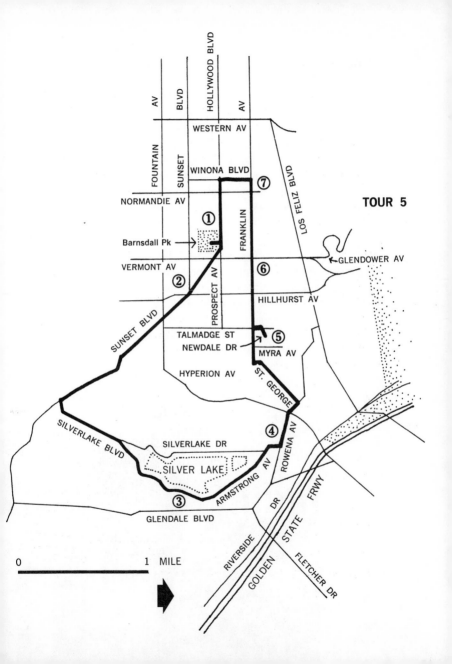

of Myra, is the better one, showing the architect in full command of his characteristic planes and angles. It was built in 1951. The other, at 4237 Newdale Drive, is Elliot House, built in 1931.

6. Wright's monumental Ennis house is visible on the hillside from Franklin and Vermont. The completely dedicated will want to push their bicycles up curving Glendower Avenue to get a closer look at this impressive 1924 example of concrete block construction. Others may rather visit the outstanding Sorbonne French Bakery at 1966 Hillhurst Avenue, for a quick-energy snack.

7. At 5121 Franklin Avenue is Sowden House, one of Wright's strangest and most organic creations. The cavelike entrance leads to an inner court, which in 1926 contained an elaborate fountain. Directly above the house for several blocks was the large Cecil B. DeMille estate, now subdivided, but still private. Winona, certainly one of the shortest boulevards in Los Angeles, takes us back to Hollywood and Barnsdall Park.

While you bicycle you can look at bike shops along the way.

6 THROUGH BEVERLY HILLS

LENGTH: *10 miles round trip*
TERRAIN: *Mild slopes mainly*
TRAFFIC: *Light to medium*
BEST RIDDEN: *Any time of the year*

Ogden Nash once observed, "Bankers are like everyone else, except richer." Well, so is Beverly Hills. Like everyplace else, except richer. And on purpose, too. One of the first fully planned townships, Beverly Hills was designed in 1906 to be an island of affluence and gentility. And despite a growing business district, the city never lost sight of that goal. Today, the residential section north of Santa Monica comes closest to the original plan. This is where Beverly Drive and Canon Drive cross neatly to enclose Will Rogers Park and the Beverly Hills Hotel, while all the other Drives follow symmetrically along. Our tour explores these lanes of luxury, and the opulent business triangle between Santa Monica and Wilshire as well. We wheel into the golden precincts through Century City, a more recent version of land planning. Century City was supposed to be for pedestrians as well as cars, but it hasn't quite worked out that way. The high-rise landscape is still a bit stark for walking. On the other hand, the grand avenues provide some of the most magnificent bikeways around. All in all, this trip is a real joy for the cognicenti, for those with-it cyclists who know how to appreciate the finer things in city touring.

Along the Way

1. We sally forth up Motor Avenue from the parking lot of Rancho Park, a large and well-equipped expanse at the south entrance to Century City. Besides the normal grassy pleasures, Rancho features some exciting amateur soccer games almost every Sunday afternoon.

2. Directly across the park on Pico Boulevard is Twentieth Century Fox Studio. The famous Old New York set from 'Hello Dolly' is just visible over the front walls. Century City is built on land that was Twentieth's immense back lot before the hard times came to the movie industry.

3. We turn off Pico onto the Avenue of the Stars, which sounds dramatic and is dramatic. We almost expect a swell of background music as we top the broad rise over Olympic and sail past pools and fountains to Santa Monica Boulevard. The surrounding towers represent the work of nearly every major architectural firm in the country.

4. Just beyond the Friars Club building we turn quickly onto Charleville Avenue and then Roxbury Drive to avoid the crowded Wilshire intersection.

5. Roxbury leads us across Wilshire to Brighton Way, and on into the business triangle. Except for Sunday, when the streets empty, there is a constant and mind-boggling swirl of stylish people past the posh shops, restaurants, and dens of finance. Since bicycles are now also in fashion, we fit the scene perfectly.

6. Litton Corporation headquarters, on Crescent Drive at Brighton, has a most inviting patio, brick-paved, with an attractive

Casual opulence is the signature of the worldly city of Beverly Hills.

fountain. Just right for a half-time pause. Be careful to leave it as clean as you found it.

7. Crescent Drive takes us past civic center. The elaborately Spanish City Hall, topped by a shiny golden dome, may not be great architecture, but it seems just right for Beverly Hills.

8. Above Santa Monica the cyclist enters the gentle slopes of the Santa Monica foothills, and one of the most determinedly elegant residential sections in the country, if not the world. The decorous and perfectly landscaped streets are lovely to ride on. The houses themselves reflect almost every style ever to capture the imagination of the Los Angeles rich.

9. Will Rogers Memorial Park is named after Beverly Hills' most famous mayor. And its formal gardens, while quite beautiful, are in amusing contrast to the casual cowboy commedian. Across Sunset Boulevard is the rambling Beverly Hills Hotel, which, since 1912, has offered cloistered luxury to the Hollywood social set.

10. A mild climb on Beverly Drive above Sunset takes us to Lexington Road, and along the first contours of the real hill country above. For a few minutes we seem to be riding through some distant forest, so thick are the trees and so secluded the houses.

11. Roxbury Drive returns us to the city. Some people say that this particular street best captures the spirit of Beverly Hills. And as we coast smoothly downhill, past block after block of well-ordered affluence, it is hard not to feel the special sense of comfort and self-assurance that this unique town exudes.

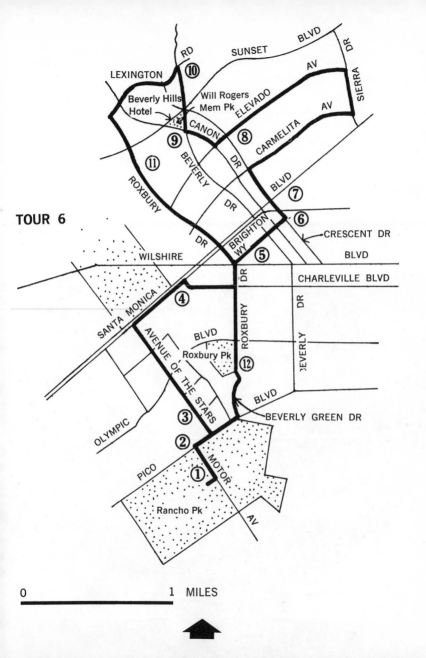

TOUR 6

0   1   MILES

12. Below Wilshire, Roxbury takes us through a section of classic stucco apartments, then past Roxbury Park, a lively neighborhood meeting place. We turn off on Beverlygreen Drive to reach Pico Boulevard, and pedal beside the Hillcrest Country Club back to our starting place.

The period style—palm tree and all—of Pasadena's Castle Green.

7 PASADENA OLD AND NEW

LENGTH: *13 miles round trip*
TERRAIN: *Mild slopes mainly, some hills*
TRAFFIC: *Light to medium*
BEST RIDDEN: *Any time of the year*

Pasadena is the grand old lady of foothill communities, and should be approached with respect by bicyclists as by all others. Pasadena was the playground of the wealthy when Bel Air and Westwood were only views from the Santa Monica Railroad, before Beverly Hills was a gleam in a subdivider's eye. What is more, Pasadena's great houses of those years still stand, appreciated, while those of Bunker Hill are just memories, and those of West Adams are boarding houses or worse. Smog has played Pasadena a cruel trick. But smog is only a surface affliction, like wrinkles. And unlike wrinkles, smog sometimes goes away. Our tour takes the cyclist through several fine Pasadena neighborhoods, focusing on the houses designed by Charles and Henry Greene between 1902 and 1908. These homes are very important to Southern California architecture. Pioneering in their use of exposed wooden beams, low spreading roof, and overhung porch, they inspired thousands of smaller copies in the highly popular California bungalow style. Besides which, they are still terrific to look at. The tour does not neglect Pasadena's handsome civic center, and also takes in the incomparable Huntington Library in San Marino. Because the route sticks mainly to the top of the bluff on which Pasadena was built, there are only enough hills to keep things interesting.

Along the Way

1. The Green Hotel, 50 East Green Street, is the oldest building on our tour, and so makes a logical starting point. Built in 1889 and added to in 1902, this extravaganza is the only one of the great Pasadena resort hotels remaining in anything like original condition.

2. A raunchy stretch of Colorado Boulevard climbs to the Art Museum, a new and strikingly modern addition to the Pasadena scene designed by Ladd and Kelsey.

3. The houses at 368, 370, 400, and 408 Arroyo Terrace were all built by the Greene brothers between 1902 and 1905. Narrowly escaping death by freeway, this quiet neighborhood is about to undergo invasion by apartment. But for the time being it preserves much of the feel of early Pasadena.

4. Gamble House, the magnificent culmination of the Greene style, has been guaranteed preservation by the American Institute of Architects, who now own it. Located at 4 Westmoreland Place, the house is reached through Orange Grove Boulevard, once called "Millionaire's Row." Cyclists are most welcome, because "they don't drip oil on the brick drive."

5. Pasadena City Hall stands monumentally at the end of the short ride down Holly Street. Another fine example of 1920's Spanish Revival in civic architecture is the Public Library at 285 East Walnut Street.

6. Colorado Boulevard here retains the exhuberance of a growing midwestern town. Around the corner at El Molino Avenue is the Pasadena Playhouse, built in 1924 and closed recently by an inability to make ends meet.

Bicycling, even when it is cold, is great sport.

7. Bullocks Pasadena Department Store is at 401 South Lake Street. Designed in 1947 by Walter Wurdeman and Welton Becket, Bullocks helped set the pace locally for a new architectural approach to store design. The result has certainly stood up well to time.

8. Our route on California Boulevard leads past the California Institute of Technology, an outstanding university, and, as parent of the Jet Propulsion Laboratories, a heavy contributor to our amusements in space. The small campus lends itself well to bicycle snooping.

9. At Allen Avenue we enter the manicured precincts of San Marino, perhaps the last serious outpost of privilege and exclusion in the Los Angeles area. One of the more interesting San Marino homes is Neff House, at 1883 Orlando Road, a deceptively simple expression of 1929 Spanish Colonial Revival.

10. Huntington Library and Art Gallery contains treasures beyond count and description, and enchanting gardens in which to stretch your legs. Spend several hours here if you can. It is open from 1 to 4:30 every day except Monday, and admission is free.

11. Euston Road starts a lovely fast ride downhill, through stately streets, which must be paid back by a short steep climb up the Pasadena bluff on Oak Knoll Avenue.

12. Blacker House at Hillcrest and Wentworth Avenues is second only to Gamble House as the greatest Greene and Greene creation. Its setting here in a viable, contemporary neighborhood shows even better the amazing lasting quality of these 65-year-old masterpieces.

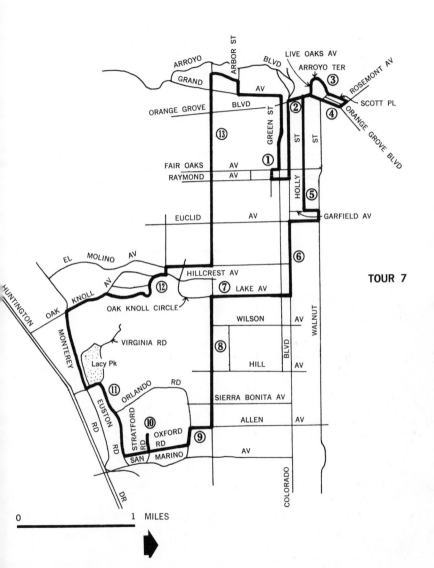

TOUR 7

13. Back in old Pasadena, we take California Boulevard to the edge of the arroyo, then return to the town center by way of Grand Avenue, along which the fine homes, including several by the Greenes, are unfortunately well hidden from view.

Bicycling, like motoring, should be done defensively.

8 BRENTWOOD TO SANTA MONICA

LENGTH: *10 miles round trip*
TERRAIN: *Mainly flat, gentle slopes*
TRAFFIC: *Light to medium*
BEST RIDDEN: *Spring and summer*

Santa Monica Bay was one of the first places to be connected by railroad to fledgling Los Angeles. In 1875, excursion passengers would travel all the way out to the beach at the foot of Santa Monica Canyon, there to spend a cool day under tents and pavillions. The town of Santa Monica grew as a seacoast resort on the palisades overlooking the ocean. Visitors liked to promenade in front of the grand hotels, taking the fresh air and enjoying the magnificent panoramic view. Of all the local beach cities, Santa Monica has best kept its early character. It is an independent place, with a good deal of civic consciousness, directed mainly toward making life by the sea even more pleasant. To this end, Santa Monica has designated certain streets as a marked bikeway which circles the entire town. Our tour includes the more scenic portions of the bikeway: along the palisades, and through the fine northside residential district. We approach Santa Monica down San Vicente Boulevard, with its lovely park-like center strip. Interestingly enough, this was the former right-of-way for the railroad line. Pedalling past lush Palisades Park, we visit the salty old Municipal Pier before returning along the bikeway to our Brentwood starting point. This is a fine family ride, a real going-to-the-beach adventure for the youngsters, and a good time for their parents as well.

Along the Way

1. Brentwood School on Gretna Green Way is our rallying point. There is plenty of parking on the west side of the street, against the dense windbreak of the Brentwood Country Club.

2. San Vicente Boulevard is probably the finest approach to the Pacific on the whole California coast. For over three miles, its magnificent coral trees parade down the grassy median strip. Around March, the trees bloom, making the display even more grand. Both sides of the Boulevard are lined with lovely homes and colorful foliage. Long a favorite of joggers, San Vicente has recently become a prime thoroughfare for cyclists as well.

3. A detour at 7th Street leads down steep Entrada Drive into arty Santa Monica Canyon, and onto the Pacific Coast Highway at Will Rogers Beach. Up the coast is Tour 10 to Malibu, down the coast is another way to the Santa Monica Pier and Tour 9.

4. As San Vicente reaches Palisades Park, we are treated to a truly breathtaking seascape of Santa Monica Bay. On a clear day, the view stretches from Pt. Dume on the right to Palos Verdes on the left, and includes Catalina Island on the horizon. Between the many palms, the Pacific sparkles like a travel agent's dream. A number of charming pavillions provide perfect settings for a bit of meditation.

5. The Camera Obscura, in the Senior Citizen's Recreation building at California Avenue, is another way to look at the wonderful view. This modern version of an ancient device is open weekdays 9-4:30, and weekends 11-4.

6. Ocean Avenue is a favorite part of the Santa Monica bikeway;

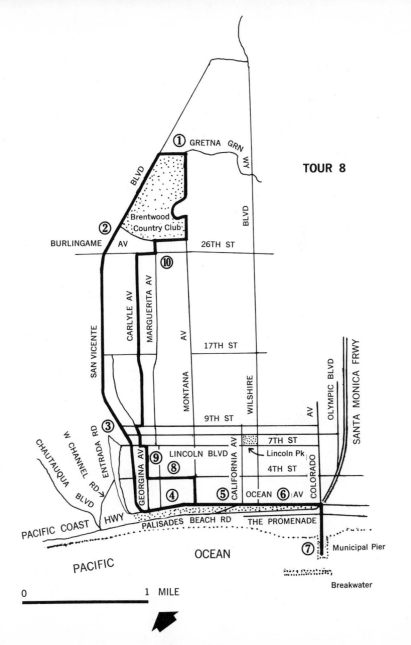

TOUR 8

GRETNA GRN WY

① GRETNA GRN WY

BLVD

BLVD

Brentwood Country Club

② BURLINGAME AV

26TH ST

⑩

CARLYLE AV

MARGUERITA AV

AV

MONTANA AV

17TH ST

SAN VICENTE

WILSHIRE

OLYMPIC BLVD

SANTA MONICA FRWY

9TH ST

③

ENTRADA RD

W CHANNEL RD

CHAUTAUQUA BLVD

GEORGINA AV

⑨

⑧ LINCOLN BLVD

7TH ST

Lincoln Pk

CALIFORNIA AV

4TH ST

④

⑤

OCEAN ⑥ AV

COLORADO

PACIFIC COAST HWY

PALISADES BEACH RD

THE PROMENADE

⑦ Municipal Pier

OCEAN

PACIFIC

Breakwater

0   1 MILE

Sunday finds it crowded with cyclists of all sorts. And rightly so. Riding between the green park and the pastel hotels under a clear blue sky is a beautiful experience indeed.

7. On Santa Monica Municipal Pier the patient fishermen await some action from the wary perch, corbina, halibut, tomcod, herring, mackerel, and occasional sand shark, while the tourists wander in and out of the bars, restaurants, gift stores, bait-and-tackle shops, and other attractions of this 63-year old structure. The walkway under the pier, reached by a ramp alongside the happy-sad old merry-go-round, begins the Beach Bikeway and Tour 9.

8. We return on Ocean Avenue to Montana Avenue, and three blocks over swing up 4th Street, a gracious, tree-lined passage through one of Santa Monica's older residential areas.

9. At Georgina Avenue we rejoin the Santa Monica Bikeway, and follow its signs onto Carlyle Avenue. The Bikeway turns south at 17th, but we continue on under a lengthy gray-green archway of Canary Island Pines, reaching high above the quiet street to shade it even on the sunniest day.

10. A jog at 26th Street brings us onto Marguerita Avenue, which in turn leads to the edge of the Brentwood Country Club. We pedal along the golf course border to return to Brentwood School, encountering some unexpectedly country-like settings on the way.

9 THE BEACH BIKEWAY

LENGTH: *9½ miles round trip*
TERRAIN: *Flat as the ocean*
TRAFFIC: *None to light*
BEST RIDDEN: *October to May*

Perhaps the most popular cycling spot in all Los Angeles is the Beach Bikeway, which runs for over three miles beside the sands of Santa Monica and Venice. Established through the efforts of Councilman Marvin Braude, the Bikeway is a lane marked on the car-free promenade, which cyclists share with all types of pedestrian traffic. In the summer, you can hardly squeeze a small dog through the press of bodies, much less a bicycle. So use of the Bikeway after 9:00 A.M. is permitted only from September 1 through April 30. This is the best time of year for beach riding anyhow, when the air is crisp, the sea deep blue, and the broad sands smooth and empty. Great numbers of cyclists take advantage every Saturday and Sunday, and it is a real satisfaction to watch them whirr by: youths in colorful racing gear, families with children on cycles and in carriers, long-hairs of both sexes, sedate oldsters . . . everyone. The route is colorful as well as scenic. Venice in particular has always been a free district, offering sanctuary to a wide variety of social fringe groups: artists, writers, beats, hippies, gays, nature people, even Senior Citizens. All these vocations, and more, are represented on the friendly oceanfront. Our tour extends the ride to interesting Marina del Rey, where bicycle rentals are available from the Yankee Pedaler, on the corner of Via Marina and Admiralty Way.

Along the Way

1. Although the Beach Bikeway actually starts slightly northward, at Sorrento Beach, most cyclists will make the Santa Monica Pier area their terminus. Next to the pier is a large parking lot, which is quite uncrowded during bicycle riding season.

2. Not many merry-go-rounds are built under apartment houses, like the one at Santa Monica. It pipes us cheerfully past a somewhat seedy area as we set off down The Promenade. Soon the way is bordered by handsome apartments on one side, and the unruffled sands, dotted with palm oases, on the other. A most tranquil stretch.

3. Skirting a parking lot, we encounter the picturesque, if fast-dissappearing, ruins of Pacific Ocean Park, an ambitious amusement pier which failed soon after opening.

4. Muscle Beach guards the beginning of Ocean Front Walk, the Venice portion of the Bikeway. This famous local attraction is named for the devotees of the biceps, the triceps, and the pectoralis major, who hold forth on the outdoor weightlifting platform.

5. We pedal slowly past an unbelievably funky collection of synagogues, kosher butcher shops, artists dens, beachfront tenements, hot dog stands, occult parlors, and what not, trying to take it all in without bumping the person in front of us.

6. One block inland on Windward Avenue, opposite the Venice Pavillion, are some architectural relics of the old Venice canal community. This arcade was a reproduction of the Doges Palace; it still casts a spell, beat up as it is. A little further down the Bikeway we find a more modern adornment, a terrific painted wall

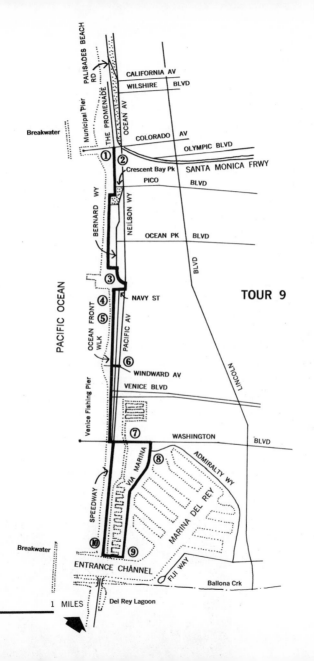

showing nearby Brooks Avenue under a typical Venice snow-storm.

7. The Venice Fishing Pier is the southern terminus of the Bikeway. To get into Marina Del Rey, we turn up Washington Street for a few blocks, then take Via Marina to Admiralty Way.

8. Marina Del Rey is a very well done and very successful harbor development, which, along with its boat docks, includes apartments, condominiums, restaurants, shops, and other sea-centered facilities. The exotically named streets (Tahiti Way, Bora Bora Way, etc.) are neat to explore. Admiralty Way goes all around the Marina for those who want to see everything.

9. Across the old main canal of Venice we pause to watch the pleasure boats in the busy channel entrance. Everything from frisky 12-footers to majestic schooners, from tiny outboards to grand, ocean-going yachts.

10. The Speedway, a half block off Pacific Avenue, is a one-way street which returns us to the Bikeway at Washington. Interesting beach houses abound in this area. There is a great deal of new construction as well, the trend, probably, for some time to come.

Sun and good friends, the big city in microcosm.

10 UP THE COAST TO MALIBU

LENGTH: *26 miles round trip*
TERRAIN: *Mainly flat*
TRAFFIC: *Medium to heavy*
BEST RIDDEN: *Any time of the year*

The ride from Santa Monica to Malibu on Pacific Coast Highway has a great sense of distance and place, despite its reasonable length. You leave the big city behind, pedal steadily on through vast, scenic spaces, and finally arrive at a quaint village with beautiful and distinctive inhabitants. It is sort of cross-country touring in miniature, a foreign experience in your own backyard. Pacific Coast Highway is a fast road, with a goodly amount of car and truck traffic, particularly in summer. But there are marked shoulder lanes on both sides, so that the cyclist is removed somewhat from the main stream. In addition, motorists are more used to seeing bicycle riders on this stretch of open road than elsewhere, and tend to give them wide berth. En route, we have plenty of time to take in the various features of the seaside environment: the eroded palisades, the mountain canyons running into the ocean, the shifting sands, the offshore reefs, and the way the coastline is formed into numerous small bays. The breeze usually blows directly offshore, cleaning the air without really slowing our progress in either direction. Each season has its own pleasures on the beach, from the refreshing swims of summer to the envigorating air and churning seas of winter. Having sampled one, the cyclist will want to explore them all.

65

Along the Way

1. Our sea ride begins on the Pacific Coast Highway at the mouth of Santa Monica Canyon, where Chautauqua Boulevard meets West Channel Road. Will Rogers Beach has ample parking; but on summer weekends, the lots fill up early, so an early start is best then. The cozy eateries and drinkeries in the Canyon offer a stirrup cup of various kinds to the dauntless rider.

2. Will Rogers Beach State Park stretches for over three miles of coastline to Castle Rock at the city limits. The large and good-looking apartments that have been built against the palisades are probably the wave of the future — a compromise between those who want to live at the beach and those who want to use it.

3. Around Topanga Canyon Boulevard we encounter the older type of oceanfront development: rows of shoulder-to-shoulder homes, cottages, apartments, and clubs, which barricade the beach quite effectively against the public. Access ways have now been opened by the County at several points, and cyclists will be pleased that the days of such completely selfserving land use are probably over.

4. The scalloped beaches just west of Topanga have close-in reefs which attract many fish, as well as the favorite game of skin divers — the California Spiny Lobster. We may meet some of the wet-suited hunters on shore, or see their red and white flag bobbing on the waves.

5. We approach Malibu along a continuous line of dwellings, punctuated by quick food stands, shops, gas stations, and whatall, most with giant overhead signs. Not a great deal of respect has been shown here to our splendid Riviera.

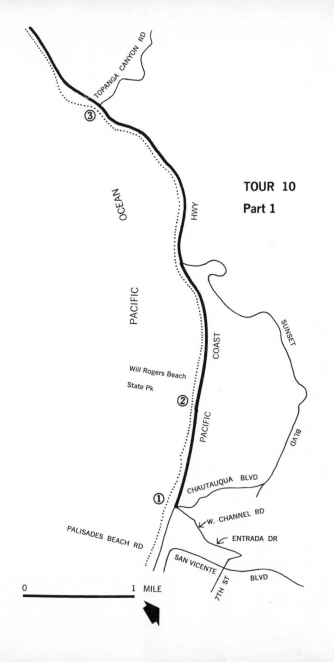

TOUR 10
Part 1

PACIFIC OCEAN

HWY

PACIFIC COAST

SUNSET BLVD

Will Rogers Beach
State Pk

②

③

TOPANGA CANYON RD

①

CHAUTAUQUA BLVD

W. CHANNEL RD

ENTRADA DR

PALISADES BEACH RD

SAN VICENTE BLVD

7TH ST

0   1 MILE

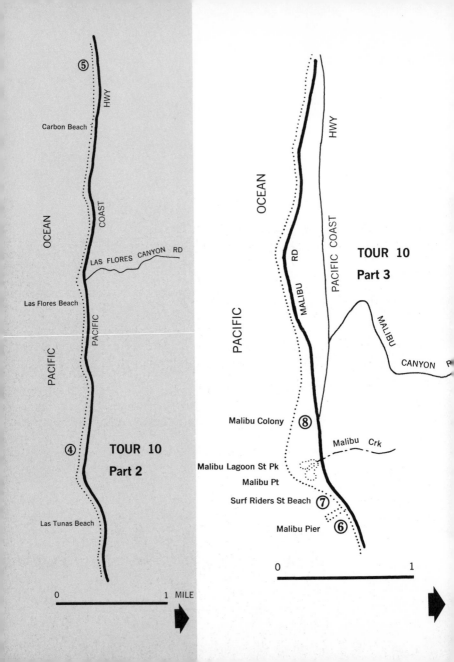

A good place to walk and enjoy the seaside:
Malibu Pier.

6. Malibu Pier is a properly salty collection of seafood restaurants and fishing supply shops. Locals drop their lines from pierside, while others take the sports fishing boats which leave from pier's end for cruises up the coast. A good place to relax for a while over a soft drink, a beer, or a hot cup of coffee, depending on you and the season.

7. Gidget is alive and well at Surf Riders State Beach, just west of the Malibu Pier. This portion of surf line has been reserved for the hot-doggers and hang-tenners, and one can see them hard at it whatever the weather or time of day.

8. We bear left onto Malibu Road, which carries us two-and-a-half miles further along the shoreline, beside some of Malibu Colony's finest and most interesting beach houses. Spare and simple Hunt house, at 24514 Malibu Road, has received special commendation; it was designed in 1955 by Craig Ellwood. The road runs into the Coast Highway near Solstice Beach, and here we turn around to retrace our route back to Santa Monica Canyon. Don't worry, the ocean views are never the same twice, and the way back proves just as intriguing as the way out.

Bike riding in the city—new wonders to see each block, plus exercise.

II THE BEACH CITIES

LENGTH: *22 miles round trip*
TERRAIN: *Mainly flat*
TRAFFIC: *None to light*
BEST RIDDEN: *Any time of the year*

Santa Monica Bay, with a coastline of forty-five miles, shelters a string of picturesque seaside communities and several marinas, offering a style of year-round living sometimes described as the "surfside way of Angeleno life." The entire bay begins at Point Dume to the west and, sweeping majestically southward, terminates at Point Vicente on the Palos Verdes Peninsula. This tour starts roughly half way down the bay at Marina Del Rey, and includes long stretches of fine riding right on the beach as it wends its way through Playa Del Rey, El Segundo, Hermosa Beach and Redondo Beach. Cycling through the beach cities is a pleasure today, but the future looks even better. The Los Angeles County Department of Beaches is actively pursuing construction of an 8-foot wide, traffic-free, beach bikeway which will cover nineteen miles of oceanfront from Santa Monica to Torrance. This exciting project is well beyond the planning stage. Federal funds have been obtained and County and State financing is probable. Nevertheless, public support is more necessary than ever, both to reassure the politicians and to convince reluctant Beach Cities that they should grant the bikeway passage. Your cards and letters will be highly appreciated by the good people involved.

71

Along the way

1. This tour starts at the end of Fiji Way bordering the Entrance Channel to the Marina. At any time of the year the sight of boats under sail can be vicariously enjoyed from this vantage point.

2. Just before starting this tour, visit the U.S. Coast Guard Station for a look at their boat and for information on boating safety. Their main responsibility is search and rescue for the nearby airport and for vessels in local waters.

3. Completed in 1968, the U.C.L.A. crew facility on Ballona Creek trains athletes for competition with twenty-six west coast schools and for the Annual Nationals in Syracruse. The crew practice nine months of the year from 3:30 P.M. to dusk. The course is 2,000 meters (1¼ miles). Home races attract over 3,000 spectators.

4. Access to Playa Del Rey is out and along the entrance Channel Embankment reached via a road that skirts beyond and to the left of the cul de sac at the end of Fiji Way. A foot bridge crosses Ballona Creek and becomes Pacific Avenue.

5. Turn right on Culver Boulevard to Trolly Way. This short passageway behind a cluster of beach front dwellings dead ends at Surf. Right on Surf puts you on the Beach Service Road and from here the route of this tour is easy to follow, scenic and delightful.

6. The runways of the Los Angeles International Airport end on the bluff overlooking Playa Del Rey. If you are plane crazy this is an excellent place to watch the big birds soar out to sea in their take off pattern. You can't miss them — they take off every three minutes.

72

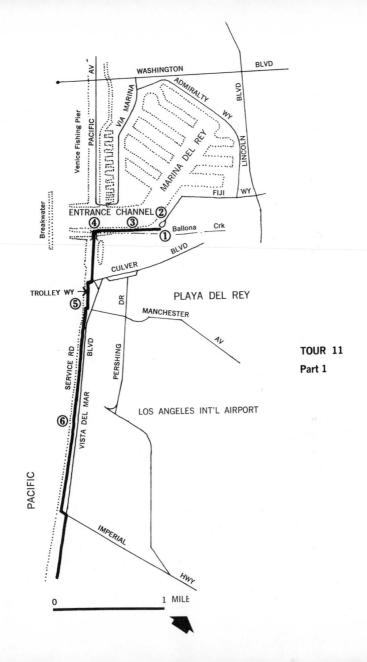

TOUR 11
Part 1

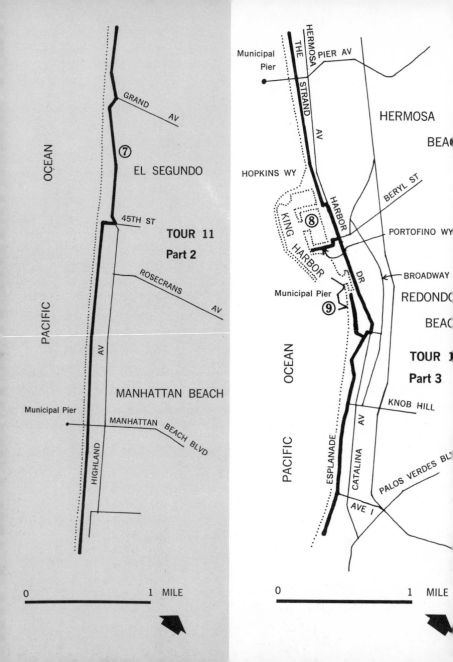

From some places the bike rider gets a panoramic view of the ocean front.

7. El Segundo hosts a huge Standard Oil Refinery operation within its boundaries. A bicycle path on their property, parallel to Vista Del Mar Boulevard, has recently been made available to the public. Recommended as an alternate if you wish to avoid auto traffic for a portion of the ride.

8. The second marina on the bay is King Harbor at Redondo Beach. Well appointed and burgeoning with activity, this harbor provides many unexpected visual delights for those with time to poke around.

9. Just south of King Harbor is the semi-circular Redondo Municipal Pier. Its shops, eating places and sports fishing facilities are the attractions that provide the continuing lure that encourages many visits. A little known fact about Redondo Beach is that California surfing began there in 1907.

The gentle symmetry of boats tied up at Naples.

12 LOS ANGELES HARBOR

LENGTH: *11½ miles round trip*
TERRAIN: *Hilly in spots, the rest level*
TRAFFIC: *Mainly light*
BEST RIDDEN: *Any time of the year*

Who can resist the lure of a harbor? Since history began men have looked to the harbor for intrigue and adventure, for learning and romance. A harbor is sharp salty air, strange smells, great ships at anchor, sturdy little boats, heavy machinery, unknown cargoes, fish, nets, lines and the thousand and one things that make up the ocean trade. Los Angeles Harbor is no exception. One of the biggest and busiest ports in the world, its many piers and berths spread over a vast area of Wilmington, Long Beach and San Pedro. Over 7000 ships arrive each year, more than 120 naval vessels call Los Angeles their home port. On our bicycle tour, we cover the docks and hillsides of San Pedro, the most picturesque and historical part of the giant harbor complex. The ten miles of route wind from Cabrillo Beach to the graceful Vincent Thomas bridge, past Navy ships, merchant ships, tug boats, shipyards, and even a tourist trap or two. On our return we climb the San Pedro bluffs to some magnificent sea views, and a delightful ride along the palisades of Pt. Fermin. None of the hills are particularly hard, traffic is generally light, and on most days the sea breeze cleans the air, so that colors sparkle against a blue sky. A camera is an essential piece of bicycling equipment on this most interesting trip.

Along the Way

1. We set out from Cabrillo Beach, at the southern tip of the harbor, and climb a small slope on Stephan M. White Drive to Pacific Avenue. Pay parking is available on the beach lot, or, early in the day, along the nearby streets.

2. On Pacific Avenue we pedal past the palm-fringed lawns of Fort MacArthur to a right turn on 22nd Street. A block or so more and we are on the edge of the bluff, looking down at the working harbor below. After sampling the sea breeze, and surveying the ships in port, we swoop down to the East Channel, the best place to see foreign freighters loading and unloading. Use a little ingenuity, keep out of the longshoremen's way, and you may get close enough to be invited aboard.

3. We follow Signal Street past Warehouse No. 1 (with its intriguing gargoyle drainpipes) to the end of the dock. From a charming and totally unexpected little park we look out over the harbor basin to the breakwater and lighthouse which protect it. Around the corner are docked the bright red and white workboats of the San Pedro Tugboat Co. Across the main channel sit the starchy antique Officers Quarters of the Coast Guard Base on Reservation Point.

4. Back on Signal Street, the first lane to the right goes past a row of commercial fisheries to the slip where the fishing boats them-selves are docked. Fishing is full time work, and weekend jobs include mending the big nets and scrubbing down the broad-beamed vessels. We make our way around the slipside activities to the one-way road in front of Ports of Call Village.

5. Reality is never quite enough for Los Angeles. So there is a

Pleasure boats and freighters surround the tugboat
anchorage at the entrance to Los Angeles Harbor.

The varied architecture of Southern California;
here, the San Pedro area.

"genuine" New England (what else) fishing village on the harbor docks. At any rate, the shops and eateries in Ports of Call and the adjacent Whalers Wharf are well put together. And if you feel like watching tourists search for experiences this is a reasonable place for a snack or a stroll.

6. Further down the road is Norm's Landing, home of the sports fishing and scuba diving charter fleet. The action occurs when the boats return to show off their catch. The rest of the day, boat owners and fisherman meet at the cafe to talk shop and brag. At the foot of 6th Street is the old ferry building, now unused except by the water taxi operators.

7. We turn off Harbor Boulevard to the Catalina Terminal, under the soaring Vincent Thomas Bridge. In summer the famous Big White Steamship, S.S. Catalina, is probably out to Avalon, but in winter she rests at her slip. If our timing is right we can watch a Gruman Goose seaplane roll into the channel and lift off for the island in a burst of wake and noise. On the way back, notice the massive concrete block which secures the bridge suspension cables.

8. Watch for the Dodd Shipyards entrance just after the return to Harbor Boulevard. Angle along the outside of the chain-link fence for a look at the intriguing goings-on inside: giant cranes, dry docks, lots of heavy equipment, and usually a number of ships being rebuilt and repaired.

9. At Pacific Avenue the easiest course is to turn around and come back down Harbor Boulevard to 6th. For those who want to see some of downtown San Pedro, a good stiff hill curves up to the bluff above. The honky-tonk collection of bars, "art" stores, tattoo parlors, cheap hotels, etc. on 6th Street mirrors that of any dockside town in the world.

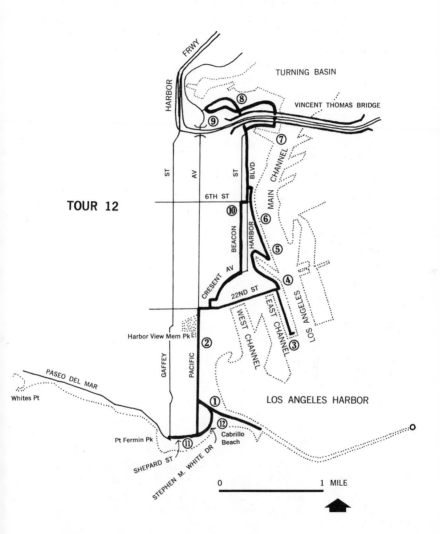

TOUR 12

10. From 6th, Beacon Street climbs gradually alongside San Pedro Plaza Park to a grand view of the whole harbor, and on a really good day, of the Long Beach Harbor as well. The route continues on Crescent Avenue, Mesa Street and 22nd Street to rejoin Pacific Avenue, which steepens after half a mile. We have to go part way up the hill to Stephen M. White Drive, so we might as well grit our teeth and pedal or push the rest of the way to the top of the bluff at Shepard Street.

11. The windy viewpoint overlooks the open sea, and a myriad of sailboats cavorting far below. A short side-trip on Shepard Street takes us to lovely Pt. Fermin Park, which caps the crumbling palisades, as beautiful and treacherous as a James Bond heroine. Paseo del Mar continues level for another mile and a half, becoming elegantly residential for a while, and then opening again at White's Point. The ride along the Paseo is a favorite of local cyclists.

12. Stephan M. White Drive drops very steeply on the return to Cabrillo Beach. Set your brakes in advance, or walk your bike if cycling straight down makes you uncomfortable. For a final treat, we pedal out to watch the surf crash against the rocky break-water before returning to swim or to visit the Cabrillo Beach Museum.

"Somewhere in there is my bike . . ."

13 NAPLES ON LOS ALAMITOS BAY

LENGTH: *10 miles round trip*
TERRAIN: *Flat the whole way*
TRAFFIC: *Light to medium*
BEST RIDDEN: *Any time of the year*

Southern California is as famous for its artificial environments as for its natural one. Disneyland is the best known, of course, Westlake and all the other fake lakes are more recent additions. But the tradition goes back much further. In the early 1900's for instance, visionary real estate developers spawned two "Mediterranean" canal communities along the Pacific shore. There was Venice on Santa Monica Bay, and Naples on Los Alamitos Bay, south of Long Beach. Venice flourished for a while and then failed. But Naples took hold, and, in time, transcended illusion to become what it had set out to imitate: a seaside village, of narrow lanes, whose charming houses overlook canals crowded with small colorful boats. On this tour around lively Los Alamitos Bay, we find that even the life style of Naples and nearby Belmont Shores has a distinctly European feel, particularly in regard to bicycles. Riding here is always a communal affair, because bicycles are so much a part of normal neighborhood life. Housewives ride to market, sailors ride to their sailboats, couples ride side by side, and children chase each other through the maze-like streets. All along our route, we join the steady two-wheeled flow. With such comraderie, with atmosphere galore, and with the fine sea air, Los Alamitos is a most enjoyable bicycling locale. And for those of us who practice one-upsmanship as well as cycling, dropping a name like Naples is a sure winning ploy.

83

Along the Way

1. Cyclists who don't mind a bit of traffic will want to start this ride two miles west of Bixby Park, in the center of Long Beach. Long Beach is a wacky mixture of bars, dives, grand hotels, culture palaces, and public works — topped off by the magnificent Queen Mary herself. Long Beach is what happens when oil riches come to a city half sedate seaside resort and half rollicking liberty port. Start at Nu-Pike amusement park off Chestnut Avenue for the old time flavor, and ride east on Ocean Boulevard for the new look.

2. The Long Beach Art Museum, at the west end of Bluff Park, occupies one of the old turn-of-the-century houses which used to line Ocean Boulevard. Museum hours are 10-5 Tuesday through Friday, and 1-5 on weekends. Just past the Museum, we swing onto the park's paved seawalk, a short but popular cycling path overlooking the broad, white Long Beach strand.

3. Those fantasies floating on the waves are not displaced Las Vegas casinos, but oil drilling islands imaginatively disguised with pseudo architecture to make them more respectable. No matter how much one objects to this in principle, it's hard to deny they are effective.

4. Just east of the Belmont Fishing Pier is Olympic Plaza, whose giant-sized swimming pool is enclosed in a modern building with the scale and detached air of a Greek temple. This exceptional civic monument is certainly worth a brief detour.

5. Divided Ocean Boulevard is the main thoroughfare for cyclists. We ride out past the rows of weathered beach homes to the jetty for a view of yachts at anchor and under sail, then back along

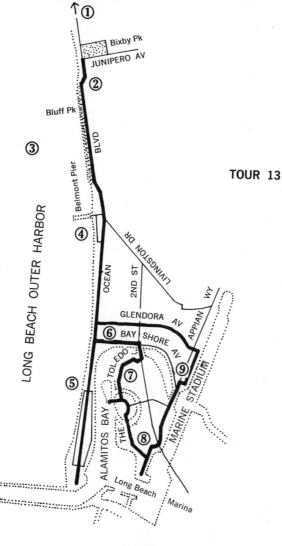

To Downtown Long Beach

①

Bixby Pk

JUNIPERO AV

②

Bluff Pk

③

BLVD

TOUR 13

Belmont Pier

④

LONG BEACH OUTER HARBOR

OCEAN

LIVINGSTON DR

2ND ST

APPIAN WY

GLENDORA AV

⑥ BAY SHORE AV

⑨

TOLEDO

⑤

⑦

ALAMITOS BAY

THE

MARINE STADIUM

⑧

Long Beach Marina

0   1 MILE

boatyards and beaches to the Naples turnoff. On the ocean side, a narrow wooden walkway runs between the houses and the sandy beach; while on the Bay side, Bayshore Walk brings the sight-seer opposite the Naples islands.

6. Bay Shore Avenue follows the beach line to 2nd Street. We swing right on 2nd, cross the small Bay bridge to the main Isle of Naples, then turn immediately right again onto The Toledo.

7. The Toledo guides us through the Naples labyrinth. We first cross the Rivo Alto Canal onto the small central island. Neapolitan Lane to the right crosses the canal again onto tiny Treasure Island, where the streets are even narrower and more packed. To the left, Neapolitan Lane curves around the lovely fountained plaza to pick up The Toledo on the east side. There are fine houses and picture-postcard scenes in every corner of this unique district. Explore it freely, and when finally lost, just ask a native for directions.

8. Appian Way takes us past the Naples boat harbor (the Long Beach Yacht Club is across the Bay) under 2nd Street, and back onto the mainland. To the right is the beginning of the Long Beach Marine Stadium, an aquatic racecourse for various boating events.

9. For a closer look at the Stadium, we turn right just over the Appian Way bridge onto Paoli Way, which runs along the Stadium fence for several blocks. Paoli Way brings us out opposite Glendora Avenue, which we follow all the way back to Ocean Boulevard and our starting place.

14 IN GRIFFITH PARK

LENGTH: *9 miles round trip*
TERRAIN: *Mainly flat, some hilly parts*
TRAFFIC: *None to medium*
BEST RIDDEN: *On Bikedays, or in the Fall*

Cyclists rejoice! We have a woodsy domain of our own in Griffith Park, once a month when the weather is fine. Each third Sunday, from about May to October, the central part of the park is closed to motor traffic. Pedestrians can stroll, equestrians can canter, and cyclists can pedal unthreatened and untrammelled. The program began in 1971, and response to it has been tremendous. On a typical Bikeday there are swarms of enthusiasts, of every age, on almost every kind of cycle. Good fellowship prevails, and the main hazard is to the smile muscles. There are several fine places to ride. Beginners, and families with young children, may want to stay on the flat, traffic-free portion. This is Crystal Springs Drive from about the miniature railroad, through the main picnic area, to the Zoo parking lot. There and back is about four miles. Our recommended run climbs from the picnic area into the hills and canyons around Mineral Wells, then drops past Travel Town to return on Zoo Drive (which has traffic even on Bike-days). It's a bit more work but a whole lot more rewarding. Exploring the real upper reaches of the park takes strong legs and low gears. Scenic Mt. Hollywood Drive has many fine views on its way to the Observatory, while Vista Del Valle Drive covers the highest and best wooded land in the area.

Along the Way

1. Parking: Getting off and on the freeways at Griffith Park is so complicated it cannot be explained by word or picture. Follow the signs and hope for the best. On Bikedays, the closest parking to the traffic-free area is in the Zoo lot, and along Crystal Springs Drive north of Los Feliz. Early in the morning cars may be allowed into the lots by the main picnic ground.

2. The main picnic area is the place to congregate. Rock concerts on the green are given almost every Sunday, with exhuberent performers and satisfyingly high decibels. There are sometimes ecological events and exhibits as well. At the south end, the fine old merry-go-round offers nostalgia in motion to one and all. And for information, Ranger Headquarters is located off the north-side road.

3. Mineral Wells picnic area is a grassy highland canyon, surrounded by trees and steeply rising hills. Through it wanders a small stream. An idyllic spot to rest up for the brief but fairly stiff climb to the high point at Mt. Hollywood Drive intersection.

4. Travel Town is where young and old alike return to the thrilling days of yesteryear, when steam locomotives ruled the rails. Numerous splendid locomotives are there to be climbed on and dreamed in, not to mention streetcars (remember them?), railroad coaches, tanks, and airplanes. Don't miss the bicycle display in the building by the entrance.

5. The Los Angeles Live Steamers are one of our saner local subcultures. These craftsmen have recreated in miniature the world of steam railroading. Perfect in every detail, the scale trains are big enough to carry their engineers over the several-acre

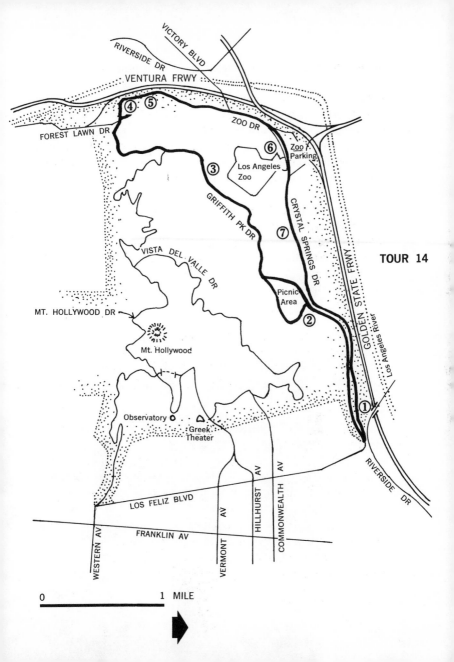

route. Passengers too, and the Live Steamers graciously offer free rides to Sunday visitors.

6. The Los Angeles Zoo is now nicely grown into its new quarters, and landscaping has softened the raw look it once had. Animals are arranged by continent, so you have to be up on geography to find your favorites. The aviary is particularly well done, and from its heights you get a fine view of the entire layout.

7. Crystal Springs Drive between the Zoo and the picnic area is the most scenic part of the traffic-free zone. Tall eucalyptus borders the golf course on one side, and there is a busy horse trail on the other. This is just a hint of how nice things will be when we finally get some long touring routes for bicycles alone.

Along the tree-shaded drives in Griffith Park.

15 ALONG THE LOS ANGELES RIVER

LENGTH: *13 miles round trip*
TERRAIN: *Mainly flat*
TRAFFIC: *Light to medium*
BEST RIDDEN: *Any time of the year*

Bicycle riding in and around Griffith Park is an old Los Angeles tradition. Griffith is the largest city park in the world. Although much of its hilly terrain is beyond the average cyclist's reach, somehow the sheer vast size casts a protective spell, making intrepid wheelmen out of wobbly beginners, and budding racers out of everyone else. This easy, leg-stretching circle tour is a nice change from pedaling to the merry-go-round and back. Starting at Victory Boulevard, where there is a bike rental shop, it follows the Los Angeles River, besides the slopes of Mt. Cahuenga, into the well-tailored, country club community of Toluca Lake, to return via horsey Riverside Drive. This area was adopted very early by the movie industry. It was over the hills from Los Angeles, which made it countryside, yet quickly accessible through the Cahuenga Pass, which made it bearable. Our tour passes by Warner Brothers and Walt Disney Productions, and short side routes lead to Universal City and Columbia Studio Ranch. True, the big studios aren't what they used to be. But it is still exciting to peek through the back lot fence, trying to guess what old movies the jumbled sets belong to. Adding this tour to Tour 14 through Central Griffith Park, you get an attraction-packed round trip of about eighteen miles, just right for a morning or afternoon outing.

Along the Way

1. Our rendezvous spot is the park picnic grounds at Riverside and Victory. Clyde's Bicycle Rentals, just up the way at 1529 Riverside Drive, rents all kinds of cycles, including romantic tandems.

2. Across the rolling Los Angeles River and into Griffith Park we go. Pedalling merrily along Zoo Drive, with the hills by our side, we encounter first the Live Steamers, and further along, Travel Town. There are model trains to ride at the first, and great big hairy old steam locomotives to play with at the second. Stop in for a delightful few minutes, even if you're impatient to be off.

3. As we enter Forest Lawn Drive we pass a bit of ecology-in-action. These water reclaimation basins are prototypes for a system which could recycle most of our sewage and run-off for all sorts of useful purposes.

4. We travel beside the river for several miles. On the left, Forest Lawn Memorial Park looks rather unwholesomely green against the dry Santa Monica Mountains. This offshoot of the grand original follows the tradition of tasteful and artistic interment described so well in Waugh's book *The Loved One*. Mount Sinai, next door, gets the job done with only slightly less ceremony.

5. At Barham Boulevard we make a tricky series of turns to get into the Toluca Lake district. Right over the river to a quick left on Lakeside Drive, one block and right on Rose Avenue, then left on Warner Boulevard, right for just a smidgen on Clybourn, and finally, left on Tikita Place, which becomes Toluca Lake Avenue.

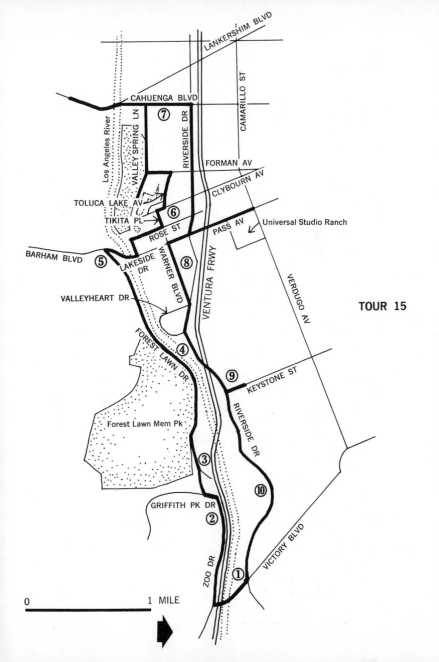

TOUR 15

6. There is a particularly striking 1930's modern house at Tikita and Clybourn that looks like the R. M. Schindler homes of Tour 5. Further into the district we come to Valleyspring Lane, a pleasant street of quiet graciousness. The good-looking Spanish style houses are set off perfectly by the country club across the way. A side trip down Valleyspring takes us almost to Toluca Lake itself.

7. A short side trip up Cahuenga Boulevard leads to the main entrance of Universal City, home of Universal Studio, and to the State Historical Monument of Campo de Cahuenga, across the way. Another side route on Pass Avenue goes to Columbia Studio Ranch.

8. Warner Boulevard lets us cycle a bit deeper into the innards of a working studio then the high fences usually allow. A peek at the Warner Brothers' back lot, as well as an interesting detour to the river, are available on Valleyheart Drive.

9. Walt Disney Productions, probably the last outpost of official non-violence and wholesome fun in America, is next on Riverside. About a block or so up Keystone Street is the best place to sneak a look at what's happening in back.

10. Our homeward run on Riverside Drive passes through a section of nicely landscaped houses, very sedate and Glendale-like, for part of the way. The houses yield to a picturesque row of Western stables, that for several generations now have supplied the horse trails of Griffith Park. Behind the stables is an Equestrian Track and a Cricket Field where, unfortunately, baseball is the more usual game.

16 THE OLD SAN FERNANDO VALLEY

LENGTH: *13½ miles round trip*
TERRAIN: *Mainly flat*
TRAFFIC: *Light to medium-heavy*
BEST RIDDEN: *Off-summer months*

This is a tour of the old San Fernando Valley. Not the historical Valley of the Spanish ranchos, but the place where our great suburban migrations began, the place about which, in the 1940's, cowboy Gene Autry sang that he was going to pack his grip and make the San Fernando Valley his home. Most of those who came to the Valley came from the hinterlands of the midwest. They were after the good life in California: warm weather, social freedom, and their own house on a big lot. All this they found in the spacious developments of Sherman Oaks, of Studio City, and of North Hollywood. And the style of life they established, half country and half city, came to typify Los Angeles to many outsiders. "Urban homesteading" it has been called. Around and through these former townlets our pleasant route winds, on broad tree-lined streets, into a fine park, past varied shops and lush foothills. The area is an interesting transition between the funky frame and stucco neighborhoods of Hollywood and the more anticeptic tracts of the west Valley. Interesting also is the distinct feeling of community, a kind of basic consideration for people, which exists in these loosely-organized, spread-out neighborhoods. Riding along the railroad tracks on Chandler Boulevard, past the deep-set old homes and tiny markets, the cyclist can develop quite a case of small town nostalgia.

95

Along the Way

1. Van Nuys-Sherman Oaks Park is an undergrown space of no particular distinction. In fact it is downright ugly. But the parking lot along Magnolia offers a convenient starting place, there are fountains from which to fill your water bottles, and anyway, a pleasant surprise awaits up Tyrone Avenue.

2. Chandler Boulevard is a magnificent divided road which apparently connects nowhere to nowhere, and is little travelled as a result. Ours is not to reason why, but only to enjoy the heady scent from the tall pines which line the way for several miles. These are replaced by eucalyptus after the Southern Pacific tracks take over the center divider. On either side, the bordering homes make up an anthology of Los Angeles building styles from the 1920's to the late 1950's.

3. North Hollywood Park hugs the Hollywood Freeway. A paved path starts at the parking lot just past the bridge on Chandler, and winds through the nicer section below Magnolia Boulevard to exit opposite Huston Street. The open greens and clustered trees are very much like those of the city parks in London.

4. Lankershim Boulevard carries us from North Hollywood to the edge of the Santa Monica foothills. At the mouth of Cahuenga Pass, the dark tower of E. F. Hutton guards the land of Universal where the television shadows lie.

5. Campo de Cahuenga is found at 3919 Lankershim Boulevard, across from Universal City. It was here, on January 13, 1847, that Lieutenant Colonel John C. Fremont and General Andres Pico signed the peace treaty ending hostilities in California during the war with Mexico. The present building is a reproduction of the original.

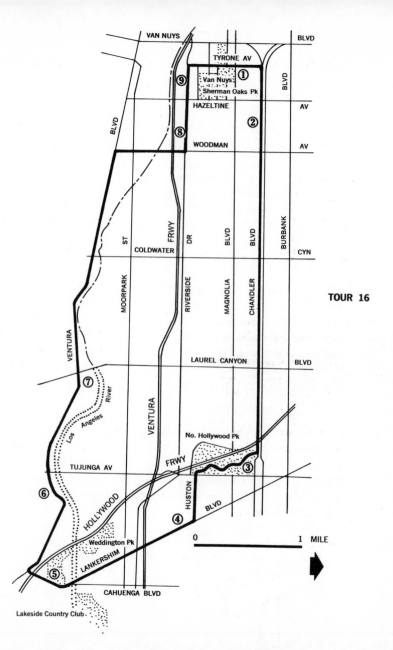

TOUR 16

6. The foothills come right down to Ventura Boulevard as it enters Studio City. There is sort of a cheerfully befuddled feel to the thoroughfare. No sooner was it settling in than it was by-passed on the mad dash westward. Now, a new growth of counter culture art shops spices the old hodge-podge of motels, restaurants, car lots and diverse business establishments.

7. A handsome row of palms leads the cyclist into the linear downtown spanning Laurel Canyon Boulevard. The look is Palm Springs, but less tightly controlled. From here to about Van Nuys Boulevard is the classiest part of Ventura. Its shops serve a fairly rich clientel, and approximate in a Valley way the life style of Beverly Hills, Westwood, Brentwood, and so on.

8. Fashion Square Shopping Center, at Woodman and Riverside, was one of the earlier attempts to group large department stores for the further convenience of motorists. It remains one of the more successful, both in terms of business and asthetics. Interestingly, the stores along Riverside Drive face the sidewalk in traditional manner, inviting the non-existent pedestrian to enter. This misconception of Valley mores was duly corrected in later centers.

9. A brand new building graces the last leg of our tour. The inverted concrete pyramid at Riverside and Hazeltine houses the Sunkist Corporation, the citrus growers co-operative formerly headquartered in Downtown Los Angeles. Tyrone Avenue actually ends at the park, but it is easy to make our way through to our starting place.

17 ENCINO TO CALABASAS

LENGTH: *23 miles*
TERRAIN: *Mild slopes and rolling hills*
TRAFFIC: *Mainly light*
BEST RIDDEN: *Any time of the year*

Encino and Calabasas both lie along what was once El Camino
Real, the Royal Highway connecting the Spanish missions in
California. Appropriately enough, our tour is bracketted by two
interesting and important historical sites, the Los Encinos Adobe
in Encino, and the Leonis Adobe in Calabasas. Both of these
1800's homesteads have been carefully refurbished by local
historical societies, and, in a relaxed way, give a true feel for
Valley life in the days of the great ranchos. We tried to find a
bicycle route between them which kept the same easy mood. And
we were exceptionally lucky. This trip has over twenty miles of
quiet streets, country roads, and wooded lanes, all just a short
way from the Valley's center of population. The "low road"
north of Ventura is a gentle rise, best ridden westward because
of the fine views of the Simi Hills in this direction. Along it are
many pleasant reminders of the farms and groves which once
covered this area, and also some of the fine oaks which give
Encino its name. The "high road" south of the Boulevard hugs
the Santa Monica foothills. A succession of suburban streets
takes the cyclist into scenic canyons and through many good
examples of careful foothill development. There are a few brief
challenges for gears and legs, but also some long glorious downhill swoops to make up for them.

Along the Way

1. Los Encinos State Historical Monument, at 16756 Moorpark Street, is open from 1-4 Wednesday through Saturday, and from 1-5 on Sunday. Its well-built 1849 adobe sits near a small lake in a 5-acre park, as restful to the cyclist today as to the stagecoach passenger 100 years ago.

2. The Sepulveda Dam Sports Center offers loads of parking, great stretches of grass, and various spectator sports. Along its northern edge, a dirt road borders the Los Angeles River, which at this point is filled with sand bars, foliage, and gently running water. We turn left before the baseball fields to get onto Oxnard Street.

3. The Veledrome, Encino's open-air bicycle racing track, is just across the parking lot off Oxnard. Pedal over and pay your respects. Even when empty, the gracefully banked oval brings to mind silently speeding men and machines.

4. Oxnard Street along the Southern Pacific railroad tracks is a bit of Smalltown, U.S.A., rooted incongruously in the backyard of Encino. We pedal easily along past Wilbur Avenue to the left cutoff, which leads to Beckford Avenue and then Hatteras Street.

5. Hatteras takes us from the small town to the countryside. Some of the farms and groves which made up the pre-tract Valley have survived in nearly their original state on this rural lane, only two short blocks from the confusion and conjestion of Ventura Boulevard.

6. Los Angeles Pierce Junior College is a good place for a rest stop. Pierce began as an agricultural school, and one will still

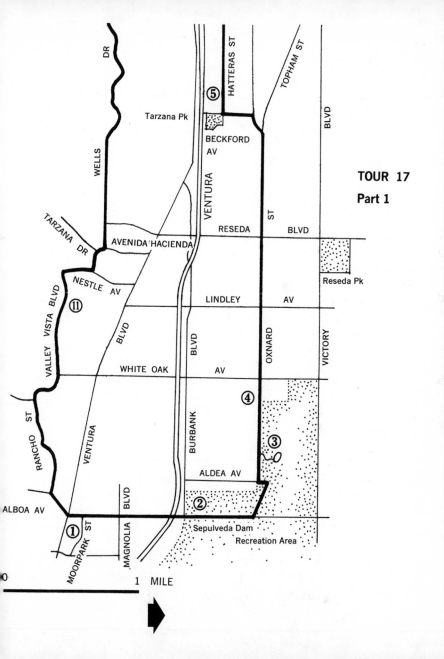

TOUR 17
Part 1

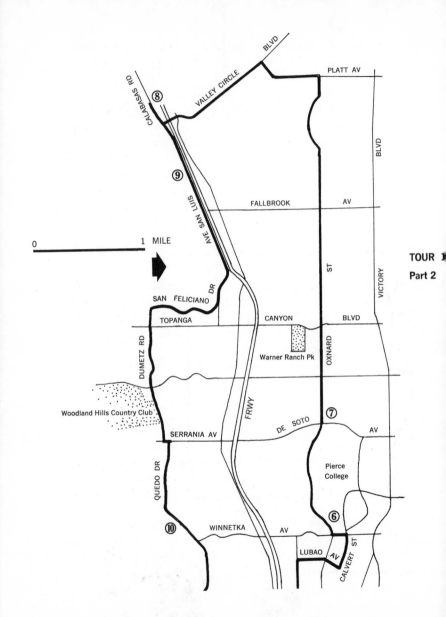

TOUR
Part 2

find orchards and livestock on campus, as well as carefully tended lawns and gardens. Only the Calvert Street gate is open on weekends.

7. Past Pierce, Oxnard climbs Chalk Hill, then descends into the Warner Ranch property, now an industrial park for the Valley's current crop: electronics. The stretch between Canoga and Topanga Canyon was dirt but passable when we rode it, and may be paved by now. Just as we begin worrying if we really have to climb the rapidly approaching Simi Hills the route turns left, enters suburbia, and carries us on into Calabasas.

8. Calabasas, tucked away in its corner of the Valley, has managed somehow to remain a town of the old west, without being cute about it. The Leonis Adobe in Calabasas is a handsome two-story home in the Monterey style, excellently restored to its 1870 appearance. It is open 1-4 on Wednesdays, Saturdays, and Sundays, as well as on some holidays. Valley legend has it that the ghost of Miguel Leonis still walks the house and grounds.

9. Avenue San Louis and its extension, San Feliciano Drive, give us a tree-lined introduction to the foothills, as we begin to gain altitude for our return run.

10. Wells Drive above Tarzana is a most rewarding street for cyclists. The rolling contours are perfect for practicing decisive gear changes. And the residential landscape is particularly good. The rich mixture of hills, homes, trees, and plantings certainly supports the affluent ideal; but the basic foothill ecology seems to suffer little from the intrusion.

11. Our "inland passage" continues through a newer and rawer area of foothill development, into a final row of estates on Rancho

Street rivaling those of Beverly Hills and Brentwood. From farmhouse to manor in half a day. Not bad for leg power and two wheels.

Los Angeles' rural past can still be seen in the foothills of the Simi and Santa Susana Mountains.

18 NORTHRIDGE TO CHATSWORTH

LENGTH: *16 miles round trip*
TERRAIN: *Flat on mild slopes*
TRAFFIC: *Mainly light*
BEST RIDDEN: *Off-summer months*

The Chatsworth area is the wild west of the San Fernando Valley. Big sky country. One of the last outposts of really clean air in all Los Angeles. Much of it is still empty; the horse ranches, fields, and groves are only slowly giving way to tracts. And it is flat, so that in many places the cyclist can see around him the four sets of hills which form the Valley's walls. There are the verdant Santa Monica Mountains to the south, and the brown Santa Susana Mountains to the north. To the east lie the massive San Gabriels. And just behind Chatsworth are the gaunt Simi Hills, scene of countless Western movies. Who could ask for a more dramatic background? In addition, the route from Northridge to Chatsworth is an excellent family ride. Starting from the attractive campus of San Fernando Valley State College, it ends against the Simi Hills in Chatsworth Park, a perfect spot for a family picnic and some impromptu rock climbing. Traffic is usually light on the suburban streets and countrylike roads; and while sixteen miles is long enough to be interesting, the distance can be covered even by very young cyclists. Pick a calm day to ride because the winds from the Santa Susana Pass can blow fiercely at times, making pedaling quite difficult. And be sure to wave to the pretty girls on horseback.

Along the Way

1. The San Fernando Valley State College Campus, clean-lined and spacious, fits well into the open Valley landscape. Our route outward starts at Lindley and Nordhoff, then follows a campus road past the grassy athletic fields and the new track facility. When school is in session, the low-priced parking lots on the west side are the best bet. Otherwise, park free along Nordhoff.

2. Rincon Hall dormatory provides homes for several hundred students. A most interesting design, its buildings cluster like a medieval town on the hills above campus.

3. Lassen Street is a straight 5-mile run of suburban throughfare, which offers for our appreciation a number of standard tract neighborhoods in a better then usual setting. Just past Reseda Boulevard the Valley view is particularly fine, with the gently rounded Santa Susanna Mountains to our right contrasting strikingly with the craggy and somewhat mysterious Simi Hills ahead.

4. Beyond Topanga Canyon Boulevard, a quiet lane of fine old oaks and olive trees leads to Oakwood Cemetery, from where unpaved Valley Circle Boulevard takes us almost to the hills themselves. The Simi Hills were once ocean bottom. They are 90 per cent sandstone, and their fantastic shapes have been carved by erosion from wind and water.

5. Chatsworth Park South is entered through a gate at the end of Devonshire. It is large, but still undeveloped, and does not connect with the older section to the north.

6. Chatsworth Park North is probably our most exotic city park. Aside from the usual picnic amenities and ballfields, it includes

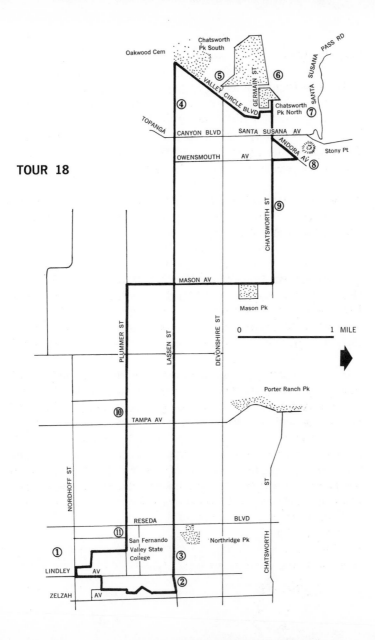

TOUR 18

hills and rocks so picturesque they seem unreal. Clamboring is the featured pastime. And if you clambor with care, you might just catch a Southern Pacific train entering the tunnel right above the recreation area.

7. For the intrepid cyclist, the old Santa Susana Pass Road climbs slowly through Western movie-set country to Simi Valley. Even the less daring might like to see how high they can get.

8. Stony Point is the favorite practice spot for Los Angeles rockclimbers. A close view of its grafitti-covered sides is obtained from Andora Avenue detour, which leads through groves blackened by the destructive fire of 1970.

9. Rural Chatsworth Street leads us briefly into the Santa Susana Foothills. As yet, there is no continuous bicycle route through this lovely north country, so we turn south down Mason Avenue and re-enter suburbia to pick up our return route on Plummer Street.

10. The Northridge Fashion Center at Plummer and Tampa contains Bullocks' most recent contribution to Southland architecture. Its pyramidal exterior is worth a side trip to see. And if the store is open, don't miss a ride on the Op-art escalator.

11. Plummer Street passes several blocks of student apartments to dead-end right in the middle of campus. Use the opportunity to do some imaginative exploring of the buildings and grounds. The exact path back is left as an exercise for the student.

19 AROUND CHATSWORTH RESERVOIR

LENGTH: *6½ miles round trip*
TERRAIN: *Mild slopes, hilly in spots*
TRAFFIC: *Light*
BEST RIDDEN: *In Spring or Summer*

When friends ask where to try out their new touring bikes, this is the kind of ride you like to tell them about. It is superscenic, just long enough to give the beginner a sense of achievement, just hilly enough to make him appreciate his 10-speeds, and just remote enough to be real countryside. Chatsworth Reservoir lies in a notch of the Simi Hills. A large and handsome lake, it is surrounded by one of the finest stands of live oak in the whole area. The cyclist has the reservoir on one side, and on the other, giant tumbled boulders and fascinating sandstone formations. Horse ranches and a secluded village round out the attractions. This ride is always enjoyable. But it is particularly nice in Spring, when the hills are green, and late on a summer afternoon, when they glow deep orange. A turn around the reservoir also makes a nice addition to Tour 18 from Northridge, which connects with this ride through Baden Avenue. If both tours are made, Nordhoff Street offers the most direct and most pleasant route back to the San Fernando Valley State College Campus. The total trip length is then about twenty-three miles.

Along the Way

1. Plummer Street leaves Topanga Canyon Boulevard and heads straight for the hills, with plenty of roadside parking. One of the last family dairies in the Valley was located here until recently. But now the cows have given way to tracts, leaving only the dairy store behind.

2. We climb slightly on Plummer into the reservoir area. This is horse country all around, and many animals are boarded on the various ranches, several of which also rent mounts for riding the hill trails.

3. Chatsworth Reservoir collects water from the Owens River in Northern California for distribution to the West Valley. It has been emptied for enlargement and resurfacing, but should soon be returned to its former glory. Meanwhile, we focus on the surrounding parkland, which contains multitudes of magnificent live oaks.

4. The small community by the lake is actually part of Ventura County. Rugged individualism seems to be its keynote. Houses ranging from shacks to mansions nestle among the giant boulders of the equally rugged hills. Watch for the novel stone house past the little church on the north side of Valley Circle Boulevard.

5. Woolsey Canyon Road leads to where North American Rockwell Corporation tests rocket motors and other things. Entry is supposedly restricted, but the climb itself is more of a deterrent. If you risk both, you are rewarded by a closer look at the Simi geology, and a fine overview of the whole Valley.

6. From this part of the road are visible some exceptionally grand oaks, standing in dignified isolation from their neighbors.

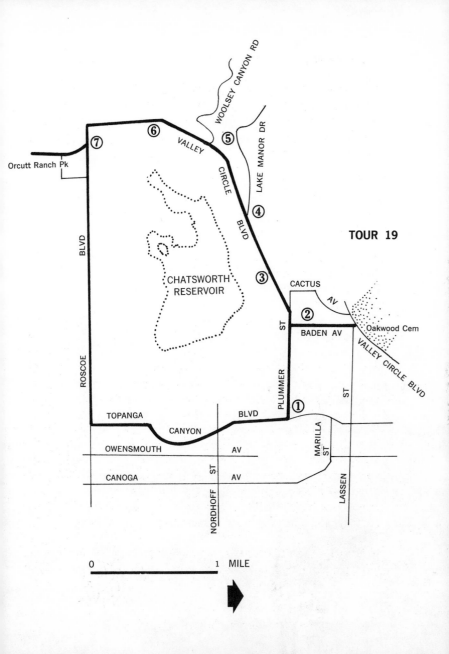

TOUR 19

7. Roscoe Boulevard is a decision point. For compulsive round-trippers, the road onward covers some agreeable but undistinguished suburban thoroughfares. Others might be better advised to retrace the more scenic path around the reservoir. Those riding the West Valley Circle will turn down March Avenue to continue their route. And all might benefit by a rest pause in adjacent Orcutt Ranch Park.

The views for the cyclist range from skyscrapers to the bucolic.

20 THE WEST VALLEY CIRCLE

LENGTH: *33 miles round trip*
TERRAIN: *From flatlands to rolling hills*
TRAFFIC: *Mainly light*
BEST RIDDEN: *Any time of the year*

It is possible to make a scenic "foothill circuit" of the west San Fernando Valley by putting together Tours 17, 18, and 19 and adding this lateral. The complete route takes the cyclist through three interesting sets of foothills, and into some fine countryside behind the Chatsworth Reservoir. It can be ridden in either direction, but is perhaps a bit more enjoyable counterclockwise, with the hills on the right. To do it that way, start Tour 18 at San Fernando Valley State College and ride Lassen Street west to Mason Avenue. Turn up Mason to Chatsworth Street and along the Santa Susana foothills into Chatsworth Park. From the park, take Valley Circle Boulevard to Baden Avenue, which leads to Tour 19 around Chatsworth Reservoir. This lateral starts at Roscoe Boulevard and March Avenue, and follows a ridge of the Simi Hills until it connects at Platt Avenue with Tour 17 into Calabasas. From Calabasas, follow the high road through the Santa Monica foothills to Encino, stopping at Los Encinos Historical Monument or at the Sepulveda Dam park. Continue on Tour 17 to Oxnard Street and Lindley Avenue and take Lindley north to the SFVSC campus. None of the segments are overly difficult, but together they provide a good workout for the ambitious rider.

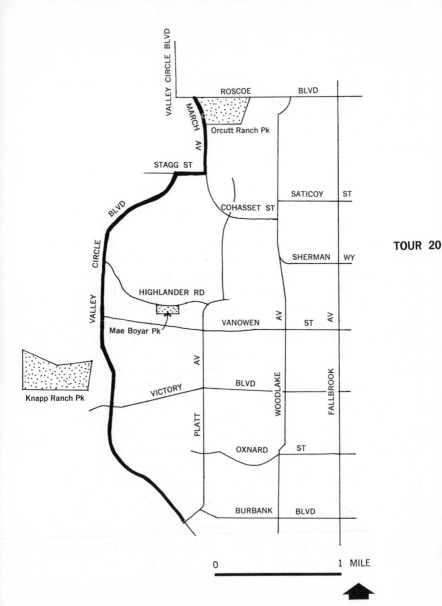

VALLEY CIRCLE BLVD

ROSCOE BLVD

Orcutt Ranch Pk

MARCH AV

STAGG ST

CIRCLE BLVD

SATICOY ST

COHASSET ST

VALLEY

SHERMAN WY

HIGHLANDER RD

Mae Boyar Pk

VANOWEN ST AV

AV

Knapp Ranch Pk

VICTORY BLVD

WOODLAKE

FALLBROOK

PLATT AV

OXNARD ST

BURBANK BLVD

TOUR 20

0   1 MILE

21 THE MISSION CITY OF SAN FERNANDO

LENGTH: *14 miles round trip*
TERRAIN: *Mainly flat, mild slopes*
TRAFFIC: *Light to medium*
BEST RIDDEN: *Any time of the year*

A ride through the San Fernando area captures much of early California history. San Fernando Mission was established in 1797 by Franciscan fathers on land surveyed by the pioneering Portola expedition of 1769 from San Diego to Monterrey. It was the first real community of the vast San Fernando Rancho, which included almost all of the present Valley. In 1834, the Mexican government took over the Mission, intending to return its holdings to the Indians. Instead, the local Governor parcelled the land out to his friends. The Mission area figured strategically in the Mexican-American war; and some time after California statehood, the settlement became a town. San Fernando was linked to Los Angeles by Southern Pacific railroad in 1876, and remained a center of agriculture until the great people-migration into the Valley destroyed its main source of livelihood. The town has not given up its independence, however, nor its character. It is still largely Mexican, and still keeps strong connections to Mission and Church. Our tour starts at the historic Mission, goes into the town center, and continues out through neighboring Sylmar to the old olive groves which border the San Gabriel foothills, following closely the route taken by Portola. For mountains so near a city the San Gabriels are impressively high. And on a typically clear day the vista of hills, groves, and blue sky is an unforgettable one.

Along the Way

1. San Fernando Mission is at 15151 San Fernando Mission Boulevard. Built in 1818, the solid structure survived even the 1971 earthquake. A good idea of California mission life is gained from exhibits in the various buildings which surround the large central court.

2. Brand Park across the street from the Mission continues the Spanish mood, but with a more romantic air. A handsome setting of plaza, fountain, and arbors in the Memory Garden cries out for moonlight and strumming guitars.

3. Andres Pico Cultural Heritage Center, at 10940 Sepulveda Boulevard, can be reached most easily through the YMCA on Columbus Avenue. Here is the two-story Andres Pico House, dating from 1834, the oldest unaltered adobe residence in Los Angeles. Visiting hours are a bit uncertain lately while new restorations are under way.

4. Brand Boulevard enters San Fernando as a broad, palm-lined avenue in the best California tradition. The Chicano Community Center on the northeast corner of Laurel Canyon Boulevard is housed in an interesting building of local stone; similar ones are found all along the north valley foothills.

5. Lopez House is located on the corner of Pico and Maclay. This 1878 adobe, with its carved wooden balcony, illustrates nicely the spare grace of the Monterey style. There was a "For Sale or Lease" sign on it when we last rode by. So be warned.

6. The Mall on San Fernando Road between San Fernando Mission Boulevard and Chatsworth Drive was an attempt to

116

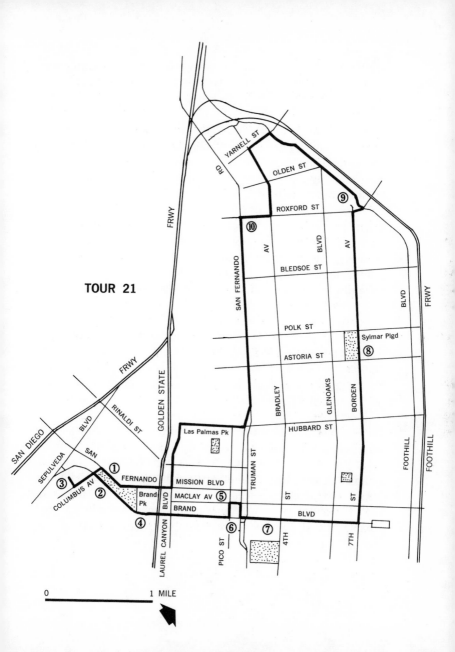

TOUR 21

prettify a fairly depressing shopping street without eliminating auto traffic. It didn't work. And a subsequent earthquake and economic recession didn't help things either.

7. We turn up Brand, and cross the train tracks into a neighborhood of small homes, some of them quite old by Los Angeles standards. The "Mission City" is a city of churches, at least, with one on nearly every corner. Our route rises a bit before turning left toward Sylmar on 7th Street.

8. The park at Astoria Street gives us a first look at the groves of olive trees which cover this northernmost portion of the Valley. As usual, the groves are fighting a losing battle with the houses. But luckily the long-lived and costly trees are more likely to wind up landscaping some suburban house than under a bulldozer.

9. Foothill Boulevard is the end of the Valley. Directly ahead are the beginnings of the San Gabriel Mountains, the massive chain which contains Mt. Wilson, Mt. Baldy, and the Angeles Crest National Forest. Our route on Foothill is a fine downhill coast, bordered on one side by the hills and on the other by the green mass of the olive groves.

10. We return to San Fernando along the railroad tracks. The road has a nice country feel to it, like coming into town on Saturday. Windowless Chicano bars provide refuge from the summer heat as well as the winter chill. Turning on Hubbard Street to bypass the business center, we regain the Mission on San Fernando Mission Boulevard. Watch carefully for cars coming out of the freeway offramp, they are unlikely to see you approaching.

22 PASADENA'S NEWELL BIKEWAY

LENGTH: *10 miles overall*
TERRAIN: *Flat with hilly portions*
TRAFFIC: *Light*
BEST RIDDEN: *Any time of the year*

Pasadena has used the broad Arroyo Seco canyon to great advantage in providing recreation for its citizens. There is Brookside Park and several other parks as well, a golf course, and the famous Rose Bowl stadium all within the city limits. In May, 1966, Pasadena gave something to cyclists also. The Kenneth Newell Bikeway, named after the first president of the Pasadena Kiwanis Club, was opened "to provide safety for cycling, an outlet for family recreation, and a method for developing physical fitness." The Bikeway is a 10-mile series of roads and streets marked by easy-to-follow signs. It runs from the lower end of the Pasadena Arroyo to Oak Grove Park overlooking Devils Gate Reservoir, and includes a loop around the Rose Bowl. At both ends, the Bikeway climbs rather steeply out of the Arroyo onto the surrounding bluffs. The experienced cyclist will want to ride the whole course, but family groups might like something a little less demanding. We suggest a start from the "Cycling Headquarters" near the south entrance to the Rose Bowl, where there are bike rentals as well as a cyclists' bulletin board. Take a turn up and around the golf course, then down Arroyo Road past Brookside Park to Lower Arroyo Park at Arbor Street. Return the same way to the Rose Bowl. This "bottom tour" is about 6 miles long, almost flat, and allows the rider to experience at close-hand the special qualities of this canyon environment.

119

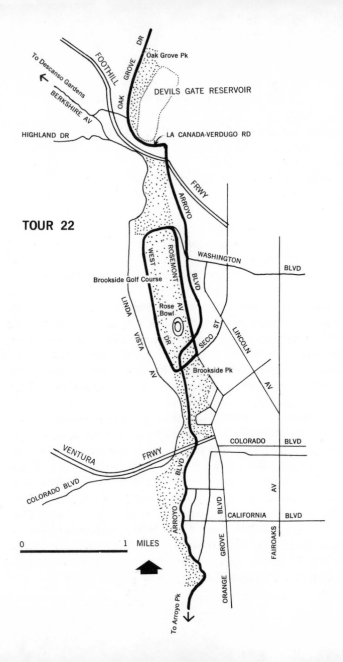

TOUR 22

To Descanso Gardens

FOOTHILL

OAK GROVE DR

Oak Grove Pk

DEVILS GATE RESERVOIR

BERKSHIRE AV

HIGHLAND DR

LA CANADA-VERDUGO RD

ARROYO

FRWY

WASHINGTON

BLVD

WEST

ROSEMONT AV

BLVD

Brookside Golf Course

LINDA

Rose
Bowl

VISTA

SECO ST

LINCOLN

DR

AV

AV

Brookside Pk

COLORADO

BLVD

VENTURA

FRWY

ARROYO

BLVD

COLORADO BLVD

BLVD

CALIFORNIA

BLVD

FAIROAKS

AV

0   1   MILES

ORANGE

GROVE

To Arroyo Pk

23 ALONG MULHOLLAND DRIVE

LENGTH: *11½ miles one way*
TERRAIN: *Rolling hills, some steep slopes*
TRAFFIC: *Light*
BEST RIDDEN: *Any clear day*

William Mulholland was the chief engineer of the team which in 1913 brought Owens River water from Northern California to the San Fernando Valley. The story goes that when he opened the last valve of the aquaduct, he said to the people of the Valley, "There it is, take it." From the road that bears his name, the cyclist can see what they did with it. Mulholland Drive begins in the Cahuenga Pass, beside the Hollywood Freeway. It follows the spine of the Santa Monica Mountains, which separate the Valley from the Los Angeles Basin, all the way to Woodland Hills. There it becomes Mulholland Highway and continues through canyons and over ridges until it ends by the sea at Leo Carillo State Park. Our tour takes the cyclist from Sepulveda Pass back to Cahuenga. The slope is generally downhill that way. But there are some fairly rigorous up-hill stretches, so your legs should be in good shape as well as your brakes. Mulholland is wonderfully scenic. On a clear day each turn brings a new panorama of mountains, valley, city, and sea. For years, the City Council has been looking for money to turn Mulholland into an improved Scenic Highway. Despite protests from ecology groups, enabling legislation has just been passed, so you might want to get a ride in fast before the bulldozers appear.

Along the Way

1. If you bring your bicycle up Sepulveda Boulevard by car, start from west of the San Diego Freeway overpass so as to get the view from the bridge on bicycle. Watched from above, the stupefying robot-like traffic is sure to put you in the right frame of mind for self-propelled touring. If you pedal up Sepulveda (and the climb is not overly hard) continue on Mulholland after crossing the freeway at Rimerton Road.

2. A short uphill climb leads around to the first panoramic view of the San Fernando Valley. Pull over and practice identifying the landmarks. You should be able to see the Simi Hills to the far left, the Santa Susanna Mountains at left center, and the San Gabriel Mountains dead ahead. Spread out in front of them lie 200 square miles of sombulant suburbia.

3. The road opens completely to the left after Roscomare Road, and then to the right for a fine view of Stone Canyon Reservoir. At the foot of the broad canyon is the deluxe community of Bel Air Estates. Continuing on, Mulholland occupies the true spine of the Santa Monica Mountains, and there are sweeping views to either side.

4. At Beverly Glen Mulholland widens briefly into a hint of the highway it will probably become, then reverts to its rustic state. The view of the west Los Angeles basin can be delightful on a clear day: the thin line of the ocean suspended delicately over the green hills.

5. Our outlook at Beverly Drive is straight ahead to the eastern tip of the Verdugo Hills. Passing Coldwater Canyon, we cycle down a lovely, tree-lined country lane, high above the urban

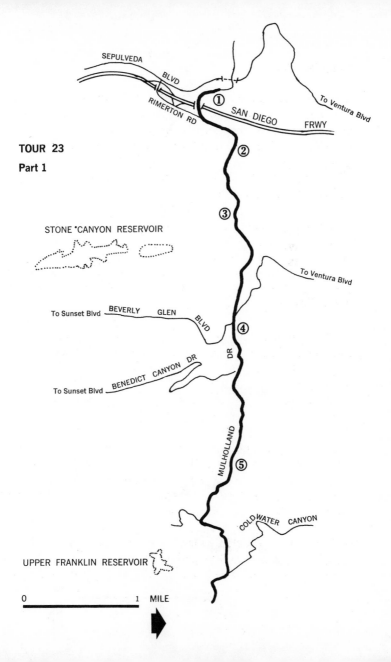

TOUR 23
Part 1

SEPULVEDA BLVD

RIMERTON RD

SAN DIEGO FRWY

To Ventura Blvd

① ② ③ ④ ⑤

STONE ·CANYON RESERVOIR

To Ventura Blvd

To Sunset Blvd BEVERLY GLEN BLVD

DR

To Sunset Blvd BENEDICT CANYON DR

MULHOLLAND

COLD WATER CANYON

UPPER FRANKLIN RESERVOIR

0   1   MILE

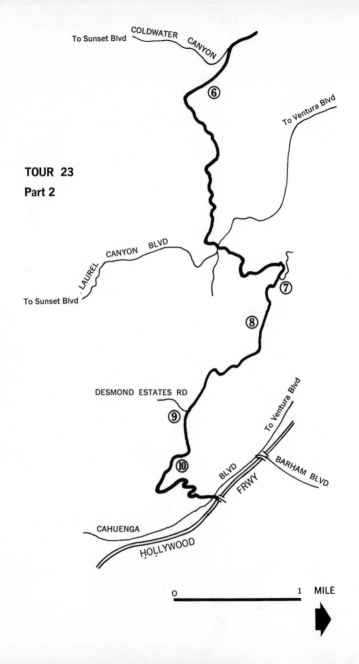

TOUR 23
Part 2

flatlands. In Franklin Canyon just below is the small Upper Reservoir, and, further down, narrow Franklin Canyon Reservoir.

6. The route climbs steadily and steeply to the water tower, then goes downhill past the uniquely plastic community of Laurel Hills to the Laurel Canyon intersection. Suddenly we are in the inhabited foothills. And in addition to the scenic views, the cyclist may now also appreciate the many weird and wonderful ways by which the hill people have managed to attach themselves to their precipitous environment.

7. Just beyond Wrightwood Drive is a truly startling straight-down view of the entrance to Cahuenga Pass. In the foreground are the white cubes of Universal City, bordered by the hills of Griffith Park. Between these and the Verdugo Mountains is spread a particularly good table-top model of a modern suburban community, waiting for some sort of cosmic social comment.

8. Mulholland becomes civilized for a while, with gardener-tended lawns and a few actual mansions. The closely-packed homes are very reminiscent of Malibu Colony.

9. Right after Desmond Estates Road we look out over Holly-wood to Downtown, smog permitting. The monoliths of Wilshire point like a latter-day Stonehenge to the origin of all this fantastic sprawl. Mulholland remains open to the right, revealing, on windswept days, Palos Verdes Peninsula and distant Catalina Island.

10. The famous HOLLYWOOD sign on the next range of hills signals a view of the Hollywood Freeway below, and the start of our steep descent to Cahuenga Boulevard. To the right, Cahuenga leads past the Hollywood Bowl to connect with Tour 4 at High-land Avenue and Hollywood Boulevard. To the left, the connection is with Tour 16 at Ventura Boulevard in the San Fernando Valley.

INDEX